Sure-Fire Preaching

One Way to Preach the Right Way

JEFF DICKSON

WESTBOW
P R E S S®
A DIVISION OF THOMAS NELSON
& ZONDERVAN

Scripture quotations taken from the New American Standard Bible®, Copyright © 1960, 1962, 1963, 1968, 1971, 1972, 1973, 1975, 1977, 1995 by The Lockman Foundation. Used by permission." (www.Lockman.org)

WestBow Press books may be ordered through booksellers or by contacting:

WestBow Press
A Division of Thomas Nelson & Zondervan
1663 Liberty Drive
Bloomington, IN 47403
www.westbowpress.com
1 (866) 928-1240

ISBN: 978-1-4908-9562-8 (sc)
ISBN: 978-1-4908-9564-2 (hc)
ISBN: 978-1-4908-9563-5 (e)

Print information available on the last page.

WestBow Press rev. date: 08/21/2015

Praise for *Sure-Fire Preaching*

As a former student of Dr. Paul Fink (1971-1974), I am indebted to him for his unswerving passion regarding expository preaching. This helpful volume summarizes what he has faithfully taught these past 50 years. I warmly commend it to a new generation of aspiring biblical expositors.

Richard Mayhue, Th.D.
Executive Vice President and Dean
The Master's Seminary
Sun Valley, CA

In this volume you have the distillation of 50 years of teaching excellence from a master teacher, Dr. Paul Fink. The author, Jeffrey Dickson, who served as Dr. Fink's last GA before he retired, also received the Preacher of the Year award from Dr. Fink, knows first-hand the philosophy and methodology of "the Fink method." Here you will find you more than just a method, you will find the passion to preach expositionally. It is a must read for anyone who takes seriously the Apostle's admonition to "Preach the Word."

Kevin King, D.Min., Ph.D.
Associate Professor of Homiletics and Historical Theology
MDIV Director
Liberty Baptist Theological Seminary
Lynchburg, VA

Today I love to teach and preach the word of God. But that wasn't always the case. When I first started preaching in homiletics classes at Grace Seminary back in the mid-70's I was frightened and lacked confidence. Dr. Fink cured me of that. His careful, text-based method helped me get the focus in the right place—on God's written revelation, rather than my own limitations. His constructive criticism mixed with an ample dose of encouragement was a turning point in my training. I am delighted that Dr. Fink's method and insights are now available in this book, which is a fitting tribute to a faithful servant of God who has marked my ministry and the ministries of so many others over the years.

Robert B. Chisholm Jr., Th.D.
Chair and Professor of Old Testament Studies
Dallas Theological Seminary
Dallas, TX

To Doc,
Thanks for teaching me and so many others
to preach the Word!

and

To Brianna,
You heard my first sermon ever and
faithfully listen each and every week.
Your love and support is a constant reminder
of God's grace in my life.

TABLE OF CONTENTS

FOREWORD

When it comes to writing I have always adopted the policy of "I'd rather people ask me, 'Why don't you write?' rather than 'Why did you write?'" Now Jeff has come to my rescue and every one's else by producing this simple helpful book on "the method" of sermon preparation and sermon presentation. This book is a good preliminary study of the problem that faces the preacher every day—"What am I going to preach at 11:00 a.m. on Sunday morning?" The average preacher starts turning pages in his big study Bible looking for that elusive sermon on Sunday afternoon. He turns pages in search for that elusive sermon Monday, Tuesday, Wednesday, Thursday, Friday, Saturday, and even on Sunday morning. More preachers than we'd like to admit even go into the pulpit on Sunday morning still turning pages in their Bibles having nothing to say because they haven't found a message in God's Word or haven't heard a message that they could "steal!" For those who have had this miserable experience help has arrived in the form of this book. If you will read it carefully and adopt its suggestions you can be on the road to entering the homiletical millennium that Jeff talks about.

In handling the Word of God there is one hermeneutical rule that I would like to emphasize. It is the job of the preacher to make sure that he knows the thought and intent of the author and the original recipients. He must always remember that "the text cannot mean anything to me and my people that it did not mean to the author and the original recipients." To find this out requires diligent work and a plan of attack that will be "on target." Jeff introduces his readers to that plan.

Jeff provides help in an area so often overlooked by books on preaching—the preacher's voice. It is imperative that the preacher give attention to the proper use of and care for his voice. The voice is a wonderful instrument. Used properly, it will perform perfectly without problems for a life time. Abused, it will give an unpleasing sound and may require medical/surgical attention. What a privilege it is for the preacher to use his voice to proclaim the wondrous truths of God's Word.

I wish that I could take credit for some of the sayings attributed to me in this book. Whether I actually said that, I'm sure that many times I expressed similar thoughts and that Jeff has accurately captured my sentiment about the subject. To all who have the privilege of using this book I pray that you will be instructed by the wisdom it contains.

Paul R. Fink, Th.D.
Professor of Biblical Studies and
Pastoral Ministry (Retired)
Liberty University

INTRODUCTION

Throughout church history, giants of the Christian faith have spanned the gamut of ministry. Missionaries to unreached people groups, televangelists in packed arenas, pastors of megachurches, and authors of best-selling resources could all be named as those God has used for His glory and the advancement of His Gospel. However, behind the scenes, there is another group of spiritual titans that God has used in an equally profound and yet more discreet way. They are the Sunday school teachers, mentors, rural ministers, and professors who train others to go and do great things for God.

Whether out in front or backstage, one ability all of these faithful ministers possess is the capacity to accurately handle the Word of God, often in the sacred task of preaching.

One of these lesser-known heroes is Dr. Paul Fink. At the young age of 82, Dr. Fink finally retired from a professional ministry of training preachers that spanned over 50 years at Grace Theological Seminary and more recently at Liberty University. Although he has not written a best-selling book, pastored a megachurch, packed a major sports arena, or planted a ministry in a third-world country, Dr. Fink has trained thousands of preachers in his homiletic lab. Through Fink's former students, God has used this unique prescription of expository preaching to reach tens of thousands of God's people with the Scriptures.

Dr. Fink received his Th. D. from Dallas Theological Seminary in 1969. Thereafter, Fink completed 40 hours of postgraduate work in communication science at Purdue University. This level of training along with his tenure in various institutions makes Dr. Fink one of the leading experts in expository preaching and sermonic presentation.

Former students of Dr. Fink include seminary and university professors, missionaries, chaplains, deans, pastors, evangelists, and teachers of all kinds. I am proud to have a place among the myriad of ministers who call this man "Doc."

Recently, I had the privilege of sitting under Doc's teaching as a student in my undergraduate studies in the homiletics department at Liberty University. Upon my graduation from Liberty, I served Dr. Fink as his graduate assistant while I completed my seminary training at Liberty Baptist Theological Seminary. In this position, I helped teach the courses that are summarized in this resource. No doubt, more than any other professor, Dr. Fink has had the most profound effect on my ministry habits, especially in my current position as senior pastor of Crystal Spring Baptist Church in Roanoke, Virginia.

In so many ways, this resource represents the book that Dr. Fink never wrote. Quite literally, I have taken the copious notes I copied while sitting through his lectures as a student or assistant and put them into book form, adding my own illustrations and insight whenever necessary. What resulted is the resource you now hold. Though Doc has retired, his legacy and unique style of homiletical training lives on in these pages and is available to anyone who dares to traverse through what Doc often affectionately called the "tribulation." Those who choose to follow this method of preaching and faithfully apply these principles will eventually enter what Doc referred to as the "homiletical millennium" complete with its "homiletical millennial glow."

As the title of this book suggests, what is presented here is a sure-fire method of presenting God's Word in the way God intended for it to be communicated. However, as the subtitle suggests, this resource humbly concedes that what is represented is nothing more than *one* way to preach the *right* way.

This book will journey through the three general areas of homiletical training represented in Doc's teaching curriculum: the science of preaching, the art of sermonizing, and the miracle of voicing. What is represented in these chapters is a summary of Doc's lectures interspersed with comments you would often hear echoing off the walls of his preaching lab that was located in the Elmer Towns School of Religion at Liberty University for so many years. His lectures, challenges, and exhortations given to us "preacher boys" are now available for your growth, training, and benefit.

It is my prayer that God continues to use these sure-fire principles to grow another generation of faithful expositors who preach out of a sense of calling, not compulsion, for God's glory, not their own fame, and with boldness, not timidity. Though these principles speak primarily to preachers, many of them are applicable to any form of public speaking, teaching, or instruction. As a former student of Doc's and young practitioner of these methods, I assure you that these principles, correctly applied, will never disappoint whatever audience God has placed you in front of and will always result in His glory.

"Let's get ready to preach them a hot one!"

-Doc

Dr. Paul Fink and Jeff Dickson

PART I

The Science of Preaching

CHAPTER 1

What is Preaching?

"I solemnly charge you in the presence of God and of Christ Jesus, who is to judge the living and the dead, and by His appearing and His kingdom: preach the word; be ready in season and out of season; reprove, rebuke, exhort, with great patience and instruction."

-2 Timothy 4:1-2

With pinpoint precision, Paul exposes the focus, content, and extent of a preacher's presentation to any assembled group. The Word of God is what distinguishes a preacher and his message. However many of today's pastors have neglected the clear instructions of 2 Timothy 4:1-2 and as a result have replaced their role as preacher with the role of public or motivational speaker.

Other subjects have usurped the Word's place as the centerpiece of worship services. Pastors are more inclined to speak from experience than they are to lead their congregation in experiencing revelation. Others begin with a topic and then pursue the Scripture as one may choose ornaments to decorate a Christmas tree. Still others neglect the Bible altogether, seeing it as an offense to many who are seeking a comfortable place to belong.

These tendencies have resulted in pervasive ignorance and the growing illiteracy that characterizes Christianity today. We have become a people who cling to emotion instead of truth, feelings instead of knowledge, and trends instead of revelation. To the discredit of many church leaders, they are enablers of these startling proclivities.

Things must change. The future of the church depends on it.

Expository Preaching Defined

The good news is that this malady can be corrected if preachers everywhere would preach the Word. Some have labeled preaching with an emphasis on the Bible with the more specific title of "expository preaching." However, even this title has a wide range of meanings. For instance, some such as William Taylor[1] and F.B. Meyer[2] assert that expository preaching involves a connected series of sermons through a book of the Bible. In this understanding, each sermon is a link in the chain of a series that moves through a large portion of Scripture. Andrew Watterson Blackwood's definition of biblical exposition breaks this chain and simply concludes that expository preaching is preaching any passage that is longer than two verses.[3]

Neo-orthodox Christianity more generally states that any preaching drawn from the Bible can be called expository preaching. Along these lines, G. Campbell Morgan[4] says that biblical exposition is any sermon that handles the Scripture.

However, more recently, Haddon Robinson defines expository preaching as:

---

[1] William Taylor, *The Model Preacher: Comprised in a Series of Letters Illustrating the Best Mode of Preaching the Gospel* (Cincinnati, OH: Swormstedt & Poe, 1859).

[2] F. B. Meyer, *Expository Preaching Plans and Methods* (New York: Hodder & Stoughton, George H. Doran, 1912).

[3] Andrew Watterson Blackwood, *The Fine Art of Preaching* (New York: Macmillan, 1937).

[4] G. Campbell Morgan, *Preaching* (New York: Fleming H. Revell, 1937).

". . . communication of a biblical concept, derived from and transmitted through a historical, grammatical, and literary study of a passage in its context, which the Holy Spirit first applies to the personality and experiences of the preacher, then through the preacher, applies to the hearers."[5]

Robinson finds sympathizers in the contributors of John Macarthur's *Expository Preaching* and the authors of other more current works.

This small survey of literature reveals that there are many varying ideas concerning this sacred activity. Therefore, in an effort to more clearly define expository preaching as the Scripture encourages, it is important to understand ten things that it is not.

1. It is not a running commentary.
2. It is not rambling comments and off-hand remarks.
3. It is not a mass of disconnected suggestions based on surface meaning.
4. It is not pure exegesis (no matter how scholarly).
5. It is not a structural outline.
6. It is not a topical homily.
7. It is not a chopped up collection of grammatical findings.
8. It is not a Sunday school or small group discussion of a biblical passage.
9. It is not a Bible reading.
10. It is not an ordinary devotional /prayer meeting talk.

This compendium dispels many of the misconceptions people have about expository preaching. One does not find the content of expository preaching through any of these pursuits nor does

---

[5] Haddon W. Robinson, *Biblical Preaching: The Development and Delivery of Expository Sermons 2nd Ed.* (Grand Rapids, MI: Baker, 2001), 21. In his discussion, Robinson adds that the passage governs the sermon.

anyone accomplish the task of preaching correctly if the end result is described above.

With this historical overview and list of misconceptions in mind, Dr. Paul Fink has arrived at a definition of preaching in its truest sense that is both broad in its scope and detailed in its description.

> *"Preaching is an outgrowth of a man's immersing himself within a passage in intensive study, finding the proper limits of that passage, discovering the arguments of the passage, organizing a sermonic outline drawn directly from the passage, and then endeavoring to set forth to his hearers the message of that passage in such a manner as to effect change in the lives of those listening."*
>
> -Doc

With its focus on "the passage," this definition of biblical exposition maintains a healthy preoccupation with the Word of God and is an adequate delineation of preaching in its purest form. As this resource develops, each aspect of this definition will be illuminated in its proper order and time.

However, for now it is appropriate to acknowledge that this definition allows for several different categories of application. For example, one can meet all of the criteria for expository preaching in a verse sermon (i.e., a sermon that involves one complete verse of Scripture). One can also meet the definition's requirements by preaching a passage sermon (i.e., two or more verses). A preacher could preach an entire book sermon and still be faithful to this definition. One can even preach a topical sermon (i.e., a sermon dealing with a doctrinal, thematic, biographical, historical, devotional, or evangelistic issue) and still use biblical exposition.

Categories aside, what distinguishes biblical exposition from other forms of public speaking is its commitment to and saturation with the Word of God—its arguments, its organization, and its meaning—above all other endeavors.

> *"If your people walk away from your sermon saying*
> *'I now know what the Bible says about such and such'*
> *or 'I now understand the meaning of this passage'*
> *then you know you have preached. On the other hand,*
> *if your people walk away from a sermon with only*
> *an understanding of the speaker or a clever anecdote*
> *that was mentioned, preaching has not occurred."*
>
> -Doc

This is an important distinction to make because of the significance associated with the task of preaching. Expository preaching is the natural overflow of the inductive process of biblical study. It is faithful to the scope of biblical inspiration and is faithful to the preacher's purpose. Preaching that is faithful to God's Word also feeds God's people a proper diet[6] and is faithful to biblical examples.[7] For these reasons and more, expository preaching is the most appropriate way to present God's Word in the local church setting.

Expository Preaching: Explained

What follows in the remainder of this work is one way to preach the right way. This work does not claim to instruct its readers in the only way to preach effectively. However, this resource does provide one proven way to accomplish this sacred task and satisfy the Biblical

---

[6] See 1 Pet. 2:2; 1 Cor. 3:2ff.

[7] See Matt. 5-7; Acts 2.

definition of preaching. As the instruction begins, consider the following encouragements.

Preachers who hope to preach well must have a good understanding of basic grammar. Distinguishing among subjects, direct objects, verbs, adverbs, prepositions, independent and dependent clauses, etc., is absolutely essential to understand how passages and verses are organized. A firm grasp of grammar allows the preacher to appreciate what the biblical authors are emphasizing or understating in any particular discourse. Grammar and syntactical issues also answer questions of agency, time, kind of action, etc., and help the preacher discover the actor or recipient of any activity. Ultimately, the grammar and syntax of the passage are a guide for the preacher as they help him make interpretive decisions that will inevitably show up in his sermon. (For a brief grammar resource, see Appendix 1.)

If grammar is important, so are the original languages. Though it is not essential to be an expert in Greek to comprehend the New Testament or Hebrew to comprehend the Old Testament, being conversant in these languages, their idioms, and their nuances helps the preacher gain a better understanding of what the original audience heard or read and how they interpreted the sacred writings when they were first presented.

There is a richness of information in the original vernacular that is lost in the English translations. It is important to understand that although His reasons for doing so are not explicit, God sovereignly designated Greek, Hebrew, and Aramaic to be the way in which His message would be recorded for the world.

Preachers should remember these more general encouragements as they begin the process of preaching the Word. Now that these have been presented, Dr. Fink's unique prescription of preaching can be elucidated. The following is a step-by-step process that will leave the preacher with a proper way of achieving a truly biblical sermon and performing the act of preaching well.

Step #1

Expository preaching is enhanced by reading the book which the preacher is studying (preferably in the original languages). This allows the preacher to understand something of the author's intent, audience, occasion, and mood through which the individual passage or verse is informed. No verse stands alone; it belongs to a greater passage. Similarly, no passage is an island; it belongs to a book. Therefore, understanding the complete work of a Pauline epistle and the reason for its timeliness and destination or delineating a gospel and its perspective is essential to understand any verse or passage within its respective pages.

Step #2

After gaining a thorough understanding of the book or larger context of a specific passage, it is imperative that the expositor read the specific passage or verse in several different English translations. This helps the preacher discover how other interpreters decided to translate specific words or phrases. A clear reading of several reputable translations allows the preacher to evaluate a range of meaning that is acceptable. This practice aids his decision-making process prior to putting the sermon together and presenting the message.

Step #3

With the entire verse or passage thoroughly investigated on the surface, the next step involves gaining an understanding of the grammar. Performing grammatical analysis on the passage helps the preacher understand how the original author organized his thoughts, what he desired to have emphasized, and the main idea. Those who neglect evaluating the grammar of any specific passage or verse run the risk of embellishing a minor detail, understating a crucial element, or neglecting a central principle. For more information concerning the process of grammatical analysis and how to achieve an understanding of the organization of a passage, see Appendix 2.

Step #4

Now that an understanding of the organization has been reached, it is time for the preacher to formulate his findings in an outline that is faithful to the grammatical survey achieved in step 3. A "bare-bones outline" is a representation of how the passage is organized along with the major points presented in the text. Ultimately, by following this step, the preacher allows the Bible to both organize and preach itself. In no way does this approach permit the preacher to champion his opinions or ask himself, "What three or four points could I work out of this that seem really cool?" The work has already been done by the original author and organized appropriately. Therefore, the preacher's job is to discover the message within its natural organization and preach it accordingly (i.e. "preach the Word," not one's own thoughts about the Word). The process of organizing what the Bible says in an outline like this will be presented in chapter 2.

> *"I don't care what you think it is saying or what you are saying, I just want to know what it is saying."*
>
> -Doc

Step #5

The next major step in preparing an expository sermon is to add exegetical notes and supplementary material to the outline. This includes the addition of important analysis on the verse or passage, appropriate illustrations, cross references, historical material, and anything else used to present the truths in God's Word. Data like this is found in personal study, commentaries by reputable scholars, biblical encyclopedias, theological works, electronic resources, etc. Completion of this step will result in the body or the meat of the sermon that will be preached.

Step #6

Finally, the preacher, after having worked through steps 1-5, must develop an appropriate introduction and conclusion for the sermon. The preacher should arrest the attention of his congregation in a meaningful way at the beginning of the sermon (drawing attention to what is going to be said) as well as provide practical applications at its end (calling the congregation to act in response to what has been said). This results in a presentation that acts as one cohesive whole. More instructions on creating these final two crucial elements will be given in chapter 3.

Expository Preaching Performed

It is appropriate to keep a few things in mind before these steps are ever pursued. A preacher must never approach the task of preaching the Word of God without first adopting a healthy prayer life. If any task required the grace of God in any extra measure, it is preaching His Word. Therefore, praising the Lord, confessing one's sins, considering the needs of the congregation, and adoring the majesty of God in prayer are paramount. Here are some appropriate encouragements to ignite what is required of preachers everywhere.

> *"Prayer is the key that unlocks all the storehouses of God's infinite grace and power. All that God is and all that God does is at the disposal of prayer. But we must use the key."*[8]
>
> -R. A. Torrey

---

[8]   R. A. Torrey, *The Power of Prayer* (Grand Rapids, MI: Zondervan, 1924), 17.

"Prayer is as vast as God because He is behind it. Prayer is as mighty as God because He has committed Himself to it"[9]
-Leonard Ravenhill

"When God finds a person who will place as his priority a life of intimate, personal, dynamic fellowship with Him, He directs His power, guidance, and wisdom into and through that person. God has found a man through whom He can change the world"[10]
-LeRoy Eims

"Your task as a Christian leader is too big for you. Its immensity and awesomeness must drive you to prayer. Your vocation is too large for you and your calling too sacred for you. But God is available for your ministry if you are willing to pay the price in prayer"[11]
-Wesley Duewel

Prayer is essential and preparation is indispensable. In fact, if more preachers would recognize the weightiness of preaching God's Word, more would prepare accordingly.

"Be sure to take out plenty of preparation insurance."
-Doc

Being proactive to follow the steps previously described and those that have yet to be discussed will allow every preacher the preparation

---

[9] Leonard Ravenhill, *Why Revival Tarries* (Minneapolis: Bethany House, 1979), 153.

[10] LeRoy Eims, *Be the Leader You were Meant to Be* (Carol Stream, IL: Victor Books, 1975), 19.

[11] Wesley Duewel, *Touch the World through Prayer* (Grand Rapids, MI: Zondervan, 1986), 216.

insurance necessary to have something worth saying to whomever God has called him to say it.

Successful preaching also deserves a delivery that is interesting, enthusiastic, and authoritative.

> *"If your sermon is boring, it is not because*
> *of the text, it is because of you."*
>
> -Doc

The Bible is fascinating to anyone who is willing to listen to what it has to say. Therefore, it is the job of the preacher to create interest in these fascinating truths and to present these truths with the sense of wonder and awe they deserve. Interest and fascination are cultivated by enthusiasm. A dull sermon is no sermon at all.

> *"We want to know that you really believe what you are*
> *saying and think it's important enough for us to hear!"*
>
> -Doc

Finally, preaching that is governed by, organized from, and saturated with the Word of God should be authoritative in its tone. One can speak authoritatively if he is communicating God's authoritative Word. If a sermon lacks conviction, it may be because the Word of God is not being used. When a homily falls flat, someone else's prerogative may be stealing focus away from God's revelation.

Where is the message? It is in the Word of God. In fact, a preacher has yet to preach until he has thoroughly examined, studied, organized, and presented the Word of God interestingly, enthusiastically, and authoritatively in order to affect change in the lives of those listening. Anything short of this is not preaching in its truest sense. Instead, it is informational, devotional, or mere tickling of the ears.

With this brand of presentation clearly defined and its attributes properly distinguished, the next several chapters will take a closer look at the process of organizing a sermon that adequately meets these demands. Thereafter, applying polish to the finished product will be discussed in order to make a good sermon great and bring glory to God. Finally, a short study on the miracle of voicing will address the glorious instrument God has given every preacher, how to protect it, and how it can be used to clearly communicate His message.

CHAPTER 2

How Do I Put It Together?

*"For God is not a God of confusion but of
peace, as in all the churches of the saints."*
-1 Corinthians 14:33

Organization is assumed of nearly everything that can be called great. Skyscrapers hold strong because of an intricate series of steel beams arranged in detailed patterns. The human body can stand erect because of an organized skeletal system. Complex machines function with specific sets of operations that occur in synchronization. Countries are structured under government. Schools are divided into classes. The list goes on.

If organization proves vitally important to the architectural, biological, technological, social, and educational world, why is it neglected in something as significant as preaching God's Word?

Structure is avoided or mocked by many young preachers today. However, this growing tendency has the potential of leaving congregations in a state of confusion instead of understanding.

A candid look at Scripture will reveal that it is permeated with organization and distinct structural elements. Therefore, it is incumbent on the preacher to identify these details and organize his thoughts into a workable format for presentation. Many of the questions concerning the organization of the specific verse or passage one is dealing with can be answered by defining and discussing what is called a "sure-fire" proposition.

The Sure-Fire Proposition

A sure-fire proposition is the statement of the objective of the sermon. Constructing a proposition is helpful to the preacher because it answers the question, "What am I hoping to communicate?" Also, a sure-fire proposition is helpful to the congregation because it answers, "What am I going to learn?"

The proposition provides several important fundamentals for the sermon. First, the proposition brings stability to the entire sermonic structure. As in a complex building, the proposition is the foundation upon which the entire structure is built. By keeping the proposition in mind throughout the entire sermon preparation process, the preacher will end up with a strong presentation that is grounded in one unique idea.

Second, the proposition provides unity of thought. Rather than build several different structures (address several different topics), the proposition acts as a building plan through which one's thoughts and comments are filtered to achieve one great sermon. Everything included in the sermon (illustrations, commentary, reflections, cross references) are subject to the discretion of the proposition. If a comment or addition does not directly correlate in some way, then it may not need to be in the final product. This function of the proposition keeps preachers from the unyielding tendency to chase rabbits.

Third, a proposition provides forcefulness of impact. Clearly presenting the central thought and succinct outline of the sermon will allow the congregation to both anticipate and remember the sermon in a meaningful way. Clarity and simplicity are two ingredients that make for a memorable message. When speakers fail to be clear they end up failing to communicate effectively. These principles make crafting a sure-fire proposition paramount.

One thing that is distinct about a sure-fire proposition is its cardinal number. This number reveals exactly how many major divisions are going to be in the upcoming sermon body. This number also correctly identifies how many major divisions are found in the verse or passage that one is presenting. Therefore, a sure-fire proposition holds the preacher accountable to the Word. Building this foundation allows the text to organize itself and preach for itself.

Another distinctive of a sure-fire proposition is its plural noun that successfully identifies, explains, or alludes to all of the major points (as determined by the text and reflected in the cardinal number). For instance, a verse or passage may have four major parts, each of which is a statement made by the speaker. In this example, the proposition would read, "four statements the speaker makes about . . ." In another verse, there may only be two parts that deal with a specific doctrine. The proposition may then read "two truths concerning . . ." This element of the proposition adds clarity and unity to the sermon—clarity in that the congregation knows what they will be learning and unity in that the entire sermon acts as a cohesive whole. For a helpful compendium of plural nouns, see Appendix 3.

John 3:16 will be used to illustrate the construction of a sure-fire proposition.

> *"For God so loved the world, that He gave His*
> *only begotten Son, that whoever believes in Him*
> *shall not perish, but have eternal life"*

As explained in Chapter 1, the process of expository preaching promoted in this resource involves studying the book (the first step) and reading the verse(s) in several different translations (the second step) in order to achieve a robust understanding of the context involved. Assuming that this has already been accomplished, the preacher is now ready to begin building a sure-fire proposition by determining the cardinal number and plural noun associated with the verse in question.

In order to accomplish this, it is helpful to perform diagrammatical analysis (the third step in the expository process). For more help on diagramming, please consult Appendix 2. Below is the diagrammatical analysis of John 3:16.

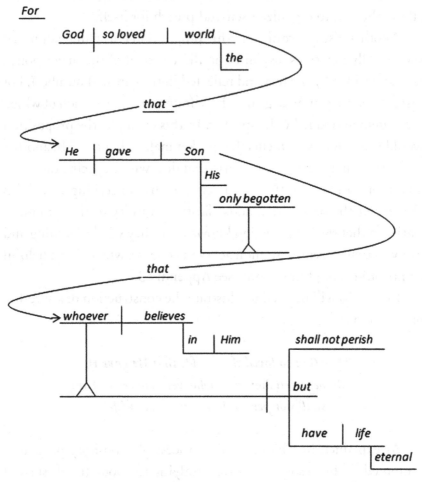

From this diagram, it is clear that the verse is easily divided into three different parts.

I. "for God so loved the world"
II. "that He gave His only begotten Son"
III. "that whoever believes in him shall not perish. but have eternal life".

These three distinct parts reveal that three is the cardinal number that will be used when preaching this verse. Though diagrammatical analysis like this is able to reveal the main points of a single verse with great ease, literary analysis, thematic undertones, movement, and natural shifts in the narrative within paragraphs or in discourses often indicate the major divisions in passage sermons. For instance, if a preacher is preaching a large passage in which several different principles are explained in great detail, the cardinal number may reflect how many of those principles are addressed. Similarly, if a character in a longer passage makes several different statements to different groups of people, then the cardinal number will reveal how many different statements are made. In these and other examples, diagrammatical analysis should not be used to uncover the major divisions. Instead, literary analysis is best.

Now that a cardinal number has been given for John 3:16, one plural noun must be chosen that successfully defines, explains, and illustrates each of the three sections. In this case, several possibilities are appropriate. Some might say that each is a statement about God's love that Jesus is making to Nicodemus. Others might suggest that each is a truth concerning God's love that Jesus is teaching. Different possibilities may also be appropriate. However, for the purposes of this chapter, "truths" will be chosen as the plural noun.

With the proposition well underway, "three truths," the only thing left to do is finish it out by describing what these truths concern. In this verse, these truths concern God's love for the world. Therefore, a sure-fire proposition for this passage reads "three truths concerning God's love for the world." This proposition gives the sermon a firm foundation, provides the potential for unity, and is forceful as it accurately addresses the purpose of this verse. Constructing a proposition in this way moves the process of preparing a sermon along in an efficient and accurate manner.

The Bare Bones Outline

The next step in constructing an expository sermon involves building a "bare bones outline." This sketch, which shows the relationships of thought in a passage, book, or topic under consideration, is crucial because outlines achieve several important things.

1. Outlines give unity to the sermon.
2. Outlines provide direction for the sermon.
3. Outlines reveal the logical development of the passage.
4. Outlines help people understand and remember the truth.
5. Outlines clarify the message.
6. Outlines keep the preacher on track.
7. Outlines lead the presentation towards the conclusion.
8. Outlines demand and reveal study and forethought.
9. Outlines reduce extemporaneous material.

The unity presented in the outline allows for only one subject as defined by the proposition. Also, the outline is governed by the order of the passage and brings order to the sermon. This helps cultivate progress in the sermon as it heads toward the conclusion.

> *"Be sure when you are preaching that you have something to say, say it, and then tell me what you said"*
>
> -Doc

Putting an outline together is as simple as it is critical. First, the main divisions of the outline are determined by the points described in the proposition. In the example above, the sermon is going to cover three truths concerning God's love. Therefore, each of these truths is a major division in the sermon. In order to help distinguish these as major divisions, each truth will be marked by a Roman numeral and introduced by its emphasized noun as shown below.

I.   **TRUTH #1: 3:16a**—"For God so loved the world . . ."
II. **TRUTH #2: 3:16b**—". . . that He gave His only begotten Son . . ."
III. **TRUTH #3: 3:16c**—". . . that whoever believes in Him shall not perish but have eternal life."

This is the beginning point of the bare bones outline. However, each outline point (of which there are three) must be given a title that describes the text found in that part of the verse. Because these three divisions act as a major support system for the entire sermon, they deserve special emphasis. In order to help the audience understand that these are the major divisions of the sermon, the main points need to be accentuated.

One way to accentuate the major points of the sermon is to use alliteration. Alliteration, or using the same consonant sound or letter in successive words or phrases, aids in memory. This literary device adds aesthetic value to the sermon. The audience is also sure to pick up on the similar sounds used and subconsciously grab hold of the major points more easily. Although not absolutely necessary (and impossible in certain circumstances), alliteration is a helpful tool in putting meaningful titles on the main points. However, it is important not to force alliteration on the sermon as it can draw attention to itself rather than the sermon content.

Another way to emphasize the major points of a sermon is parallelism. Parallelism is the literary device that uses similar structures, patterns, or phrases, to emphasize thoughts or ideas. In the same way alliteration will acquire the audience's attention, parallelism will assure the audience that what is being stated is the next major point (because it is parallel to the previous major points). Parallelism also cultivates unity in the sermon and smoothness in presentation. This tool is more important than alliteration when assigning titles for the major points.

In order to illustrate parallelism and alliteration in the major outline, both are applied to the John 3:16 example as follows:

> I. **TRUTH #1: GOD LOVES THE WORLD-3:16a**—"For God so loved the World . . ."
> II. **TRUTH #2: GOD'S LOVE IS WITNESSED IN HIS GIFT-3:16b**—". . . that He gave His only begotten Son . . ."
> III. **TRUTH #3: GOD'S LOVE RESULTS IN ETERNAL LIFE FOR ALL WHO BELIEVE—3:16c**—". . . that whoever believes in Him, shall not perish, but have eternal life."

Both parallelism and alliteration are used here in order to emphasize the main points of the sermon. Each point begins with the "G" in "God," and all three points are parallel simple sentences that are stated as truths. These titles are stated as truths because the proposition formulated for this sermon called for "three truths." If the proposition had said "three questions," then each of the major division titles would have been stated as questions. If the proposition had said "three conditions," then each of the major division titles would have been introduced by "if."

It is imperative that the major divisions be consistent with the proposition in both the number of major points (as determined by the cardinal number) and the way they are stated (as determined by the plural noun). It is also important to make sure that each of the major outline titles adequately illustrate or explain its part of the verse.

Now that the major divisions of the outline have been fixed onto the sermonic structure (as major supporting beams would in a large building), supporting elements and developing points can be added. The passage or verse the preacher is preaching will determine the extent to which the major ideas are divided and subdivided. To determine natural ways the main points may be subdivided, the preacher needs to observe the segment of the verse that each major point addresses and make choices based on what he sees happening structurally and grammatically.

As the preacher develops the outline, each point or sub-point needs to be given a title that distinguishes that part of the sermon in some meaningful way. It is not necessary that the sub-points be parallel or that they exist in alliteration. However, the preacher must understand that when a subdivision is inserted, a larger piece is being broken up into at least two smaller pieces. For instance, if someone cuts something in half, they do so because the whole is too big to handle on its own. After it is cut, he or she is left with two more manageable pieces. Do not place subdivisions unless the larger unit is being cut into at least two separate pieces.

> *"If it has a 1, it must have a 2. If it*
> *has an A it must have a B."*
>
> -Doc

When the preacher is making these choices, indentions and proper bulleted distinctions must be given to show where supporting points are being made. A helpful guide for bulleting and indention is shown below. Notice, these recommendations are different from most computer default settings. The system demonstrated below is preferable to many defaults because of its consistency to alternate between numerals and letters instead of using all kinds of symbols or bullet styles. Also, notice that each sub-division is indented a quarter of an inch beyond the greater division that it modifies.

I. **MAJOR POINT**
  A. **Sub-Point**
    1. **Sub-Sub-point**
      a. **etc.**
        1)
          a)
            1]
              a]
                1}
                  a}

Finally, it is important to distinguish what parts of the verse each point, sub-point, or sub-sub-point, is dealing with. Every "beam" of the outline needs to include versification or the verse number for that particular text. However, the only time the preacher needs to include the verse text is when the outline is most detailed (the most exhaustive sub-point that occurs farthest to the right of the outline).

With all of these things in mind, an example of a bare-bones outline for John 3:16 is shown below. The outline is a product of the choices that were made based on the grammatical and structural cues from the text itself.

Proposition: 3 TRUTHS concerning God's love for the world from John 3:16.

I. **TRUTH #1: GOD LOVES THE WORLD-3:16a-c**
  A. **The One Who Loves—3:16a**—"For God . . ."
  B. **The Nature of His Love—3:16b**—". . . so loved . . ."
  C. **The Object of His Love—3:16c**—". . . the World . . ."

II. **TRUTH #2: GOD'S LOVE IS WITNESSED IN HIS GIFT-3:16d-e**
  A. **The Act of Giving—3:16d**—". . . that He gave . . ."

B. The Gift Given—3:16e—". . . His only begotten Son . . ."

III. TRUTH #3: GOD'S LOVE RESULTS IN ETERNAL LIFE FOR ALL WHO BELIEVE—3:16f-h
A. The Condition Placed on the Benefit—3:16f—". . . that whoever believes in Him . . ."
B. The Benefit Described—3:16g-h
  1. Negatively—3:16g—". . . shall not perish . . ."
  2. Positively—3:16h—". . . but have eternal life . . ."

The outline shown above accurately explains the text of John 3:16 in a meaningful, unified, and interesting way. Notice that every time a subdivision is necessary, at least two divided parts are presented. Every outline point adequately explains the part of the verse that is being dealt with and the versification for every outline point designates the verse segment accordingly. For aesthetic reasons and ease of reading, the outline titles have been bolded and the verse text left un-bolded. Finally, the text of the verse is only present in the most detailed elements of the outline. This organizational presentation satisfies the bare-bones outline of a sermon that might be given on John 3:16.

The Sermon Manuscript

With the foundation set and the steel beams in place, the major supporting structure of the sermon is now complete. The next task of the preacher involves inserting his comments, illustrations, and reflections onto the bare-bones outline wherever they apply (as a builder would paint and furnish a new building). One way of filling in the existing structure is to insert "notes" under the outline point they modify as a paragraph that is un-bolded and single-spaced. This allows the outline of the sermon to stand out and keeps the eye of the preacher from getting lost.

Ultimately, the sermon manuscript is the bare-bones outline with all of the comments that will be presented as part of the sermon added to it. An example of a simple sermon manuscript for John 3:16 is shown below. What is presented here is a product of grammatical, theological, and contextual analysis along with the consultation of several commentaries and other resources.

Proposition: 3 TRUTHS concerning God's love for the world from John 3:16.

    I. TRUTH #1: GOD LOVES THE WORLD-3:16a-c
    II. TRUTH #2: GOD'S LOVE IS WITNESSED IN HIS GIFT-3:16d-e
    III. TRUTH #3: GOD'S LOVE RESULTS IN ETERNAL LIFE FOR ALL WHO BELIEVE—3:16f-h

I. TRUTH #1: GOD LOVES THE WORLD-3:16a-c

A. The One Who Loves—3:16a—"For God . . ."

> Note: "For" here suggests that this next passage explains the reason that God made eternal life available (see 3:1ff). Now that Jesus and Nicodemus have had their conversation, John, the apostle and writer of this Gospel, picks up the passage and explains for all who read it what this conversation has just revealed. It is no small thing that God has even made rebirth possible. In light of all that the world has done against God and how far it has fallen, Nicodemus and many others who read this passage may wonder, "How is it possible that God would give men and women new life when they have spent their first life in total sin and wickedness?" John's

answer to this question and clarification in verse 16 have made this verse one of the most popular verses in all of Scripture.

Illustration: God's program of salvation was an unexpected gift—given totally out of unconditional love for the world, not because the world deserved it, but because of His great love for humanity.

B. The Nature of His Love—3:16b—". . . so loved . . ."

Note: This widely quoted verse is the only place in John where God the Father is said to "love" the world. However, the Old Testament makes it abundantly clear that God loves all that He has made, especially His people (Ex. 34:6-7; Deut. 7:7-8; Hos. 11:1-1-4, 8-11). Here, it is the unimaginable love of God that acts as the motivation for His program of salvation and rebirth. God's love is different from the love experienced in the world. It is not trivial or mundane. Instead, the word "so" reveals that His love is of a high degree. God's love is a passionate love deserving of importance and vitality. God's love is not only personal; it is supreme. "So" emphasizes the intensity and greatness of His love.

"loved"-(Aorist, Active, Indicative, 3rd Person, Singular, αγαπαω, Constative) This verb shows that in the act of sending His son, God is loving. This word for love in the original language is a deep-seated love based on an appreciation for that which is loved and is normally associated with some kind of action or sacrifice.

Illustration: Although one cannot adequately compare anything to the love of God, a fitting analogy might be the difference one sees between the love I have for things and my love for my wife. I love Dr. Pepper, the theatre, Mexican food, etc. But, you will be happy to know that I SO LOVE my wife with a deep-seated appreciation that runs deeper than my love for these other more trivial things. This, in a small way, describes the difference between God's love for those who inhabit the world and His love for all other created things.

C. The Object of His Love—3:16c—". . . the World . . ."

Note: God's love does not limit itself to a particular group of people or exclusive nation. The word "world" expresses the universal character of God's love. God's love does not extend merely to Israel, but to "the world," that is, sinful humanity. This is the shocking truth of this popular verse—that God would choose to love such a wretched group of people to this degree. Here is how John describes the world elsewhere.

1 John 5:19—*"The whole world lies under the sway of the wicked one"*

John 18:36—*"Jesus answered, 'my kingdom is not of this world . . .'"*

1 John 2:15-17—*"Do not love the world or the things in the world. If anyone loves the world, the love of the Father is not in him. For all that is in the world—the*

> *lust of the flesh, the lust of the eyes, and the pride of life—is not of the Father but is of the world. And the world is passing away, . . ."*

Note: The world is an unlovely place. In fact, God's people are even called to hate it! Although God's people are ordered to keep from loving the world, God did not keep Himself from loving the unlovable. Despite her sin, betrayal, and constant adultery against Him, God has found it within Himself to love the world.

Transition: Now that we understand something of God's love, let us examine the second truth of this verse which reveals God's love in action.

II. TRUTH #2: GOD'S LOVE IS WITNESSED IN HIS GIFT-3:16d-e

A. The Act of Giving-3:16d—". . . that He gave . . ."

"gave"-(Aorist, Active, Indicative 3rd Person, Singular, διδωμι-Constative)

Note: How great was God's love for the world?—So great that He gave humanity a gift. His action was based on His will and not on anything the world could have done. God did not sell or lend this gift; He freely gave it. The act of giving (like "love" earlier) also emphasizes the idea of sacrifice. This is so profoundly contrary to how we think. You and I would never give a gift to our sworn enemy or someone who had betrayed us over and over again.

29

(Needless to say, they would probably be stricken from the gift list for that year or forever) However, in His supreme divinity, God shows that He is capable and willing to demonstrate His great love for the world by giving it a gift. But, He does not give just any gift; He gives the greatest gift of all!

B. The Gift Given—3:16e—"... His only begotten Son ..."

Note: God's love is expressed in the giving of His most priceless and prized possession, His only Son. This reinforces the extent and intensity of His love. The Son, understood here, is Jesus Christ. Ultimately, the giving up of His Son ends at the point of death on the cross. In fact, the grammar of this verse very much suggests the idea of sacrifice. God sacrificed His Son out of His unquenchable love for the world.

Illustration: How many of you can say that you have given one of your prized possessions to someone who actively curses your name? How many of you have sacrificed the very best you have for someone who hated you? God did. God reserved His greatest gift (His Son) for the most underserving recipient (the world). God was willing to sacrifice that which was most precious to Him for a world that was bent against Him.

Transition: So what does this mean to us? The third truth expressed in this verse answers this very important question.

III. TRUTH #3: GOD'S LOVE RESULTS IN ETERNAL LIFE FOR ALL WHO BELIEVE—3:16f-h

A. The Condition Placed on the Benefit—3:16f—". . . that whoever believes in Him . . ."

> Note: What follows in this passage is what those who accept God's gift can expect. The benefit of God's love through Jesus Christ is only experienced by those who "believe" in Him. The word "believe" means to consider true or to place faith and trust in. It is not enough to have knowledge *of* Christ; it is necessary to have trust and saving faith *in* Christ. Naturally, to believe in what is offered in Jesus is to disbelieve in what the world can offer. To trust in Jesus' coming and sacrifice is to distrust in the world's insufficiency and lies. To have faith in the satisfaction that only Jesus can provide is to recognize how unsatisfactory the world is. To believe in Jesus involves turning away from what is presently stealing our attention and giving full focus to Him.

B. The Benefit Described—3:16g-h

1. Negatively—3:16g—". . . shall not perish . . ."

> Note: There are two stark alternatives that are introduced in the purpose clause of this verse. John suggests that there is no middle ground. Failure to trust in Jesus=perishing. Willingness to trust in Jesus =life.

"perish"-(Aorist, Middle, Subjunctive, 3rd Person, Singular, απολλυμι-Purpose) This means "being destroyed."

Note: Anyone who believes in Jesus Christ is saved from the eternal destiny of ruin in hell separated from God and His love. In essence, hell is the outcome which is avoidable only through Jesus Christ. Because of His love for the world, God gave His Son in order to provide a way of escaping the gruesome destiny we all deserve. Also, turning to God's Son involves choosing a life of focus and clear direction instead of losing our way and being unaware of our life's purpose and mission.

2. Positively—3:16h—". . . but have everlasting life . . ."

Note: In contrast to the first alternative, believing in Jesus and responding positively to the enormous love of God will result in everlasting life! Eternal life is a new quality of life, which a believer possesses presently and will possess forever. It speaks not only of life after death, but an eternal quality of life that begins at the point of salvation. "Life" does not only denote active existence but a value of existence greater than what is presently experienced. It is the antithesis of existence in hell for all eternity. What an amazing provision of the love of God!

Although this is not the only way to prepare an expository sermon, those who follow this regimen of laying a foundational sure-fire proposition, constructing a bare-bones outline, and filling in a sermon manuscript will achieve a well-organized, unified, and logical sermonic structure that is determined by and saturated with God's Word. Sermons constructed in this way are strong because they are grounded in a firm foundation. They are powerful because God's Word is allowed to speak for itself. They are memorable because they are easy to follow and leave little room for confusion. They are aesthetically pleasing because they incorporate design.

CHAPTER 3

How Does It Start? Finish?

*"For from Him and through Him and to Him are
all things. To Him be the glory forever. Amen"*

-Romans 11:36

A pithy quote from a renowned pastor and communicator speaks profoundly to the topic of this chapter.

*"Your direction, not your intention,
determines your destination"*

-Andy Stanley

Intentions matter very little in life or in sermon preparation. Although pastors intend to preach well-prepared sermons, often a dull or unfocused homily results because they do not set a proper direction in their introduction. Also, many pastors would not recognize their sermon's destination if it smacked them in the face because they do not know how to craft a fitting conclusion.

With a working outline of the passage in place and explanatory notes added, the only thing left to do in the sermon-preparation process is to insert an introduction and conclusion. Although the last to be completed, these final elements are essential to presenting God's Word interestingly, purposefully, and effectively. For this reason, this final stage of sermon preparation deserves its own chapter.

Introductions

Introductions are paramount. Whether it is being introduced to your girlfriend's parents, a professor, or employer, first impressions offer weighty implications. The same is true of an introduction to a sermon. In fact, although parents, professors, and employers are important, nothing could be weightier than the Word of God and its principles. For this reason, sermon introductions demand special attention and instructions.

Purpose

The purpose of a good introduction is simple. First, introductions arouse interest in what is going to be preached by meeting people where they are and drawing them into what the preacher is going to say. To arouse this kind of interest in the sermon, the preacher must ask and answer these revealing questions as he begins to construct the introduction.

1. Is what I am going to say worth the congregation's time?
2. Is what I am going to say up to date?
3. Is what I am going to say practical?

Congregations desire something worthwhile to hear and will doze off or refrain from coming altogether if the preacher is not . . . preaching. Likewise, people hope to hear how the Word of God is relevant to their own context and can be applied to their lives. Therefore, if a preacher cannot answer "yes" to these questions, then he is already in danger of preaching a mediocre sermon.

Another purpose of a thoughtful introduction is to prepare the audience for what is going to be revealed in the body of the sermon. The preacher must help the audience apprehend the truth that will be presented by introducing the truth in a thoughtful and creative way.

Preachers also need to demonstrate appreciation for these truths and demand that those listening consider the truths as significant to their lives. In so doing, the preacher plants the seed that will be harvested in the conclusion. When a preacher is committed to preparing his audience this way, the sermon will be successful.

Qualities

Good introductions do not happen quickly, nor do they create themselves. Although the text guided the process along in the body of the sermon that was discussed in the previous chapter, the introduction and conclusion are left up to the preacher himself. This means that the preacher must decide what he is going to say and how he is going to say it on his own. A helpful tip in formulating an introduction is to write it out verbatim so that the words and tone can be presented with pinpoint precision.

Effective introductions are presented with conviction and confidence. In fact, if conviction and confidence are lacking in the introduction, people will automatically assume that the sermon itself lacks conviction and confidence. How the preacher says what he says in the introduction will set the tone for the entire sermon. Not only does this apply to the tone of the introduction, but it also applies to the organization. If the introduction is simple and easy for people to follow, then the audience will expect the sermon to be as well. Similarly, if the introduction transitions well to the body, then the sermon will move along naturally and keep people from wondering where the speaker is heading. On the other hand, if the introduction is chaotic and sporadic, then the congregation will be lost before the sermon even gets underway.

Variety is another important quality in introducing a sermon. If the congregation is consistently introduced to God's Word the same way every single week, then the preacher runs the risk of having the people tune out or grow disinterested in what is being said. Variety in the introduction helps keep interest and excitement alive among those listening week after week.

Components

Several fundamental components need to be present in every introduction. First, the introduction must include interesting material that intrigues the audience. Below are several ways the preacher might cultivate interest in the upcoming sermon.

1. Capitalize on special occasions.
2. Provide historical background.
3. Review the prior passages.
4. Discuss geographical settings.
5. Give biographical sketches.
6. Talk about circumstances of the text.
7. Address the situation of the congregation.
8. Mention current events.
9. Describe personal experiences.
10. Present helpful videos.
11. Connect the text to one's context.

All of these can be used to create interest in the sermon and introduce a passage properly.

Second, the relevance and importance of the text being presented must be indicated. Notice, the relevance and importance are not created by the pastor. The Bible (which is timeless and inherent in all of its parts) is relevant and important all on its own.[12] Therefore, it is the task of the preacher to draw attention to the relevance and significance of the specific passage for that Sunday. Shining a light

---

[12] 2 Tim. 3:16.

on the Word in this way keeps the Word as the centerpiece of the sermon and the worship service.

Third, every sermon introduction must include the major subject that is going to be delineated. More often than not, the subject will be introduced by the statement of the proposition at the very end of the introduction and beginning of the body. A clear statement of the subject, as found in the proposition will help the congregation understand what they can expect to learn and how the sermon will be focused.

The text the preacher has chosen to use must also be included. Although all of the text does not have to be read at one time at the beginning of the sermon, especially if it covers an especially lengthy passage, it is important to at least give the Scripture reference more than once so the congregation can follow along on their own. Providing the Scripture and explaining its connection to the subject helps keep the audience and the preacher on the same page. If the people and the preacher do not begin on the same page, the entire sermon will suffer.

Ultimately, the introduction is connected to the body of the sermon through the sure-fire proposition. Like hitches on a train or truck, the proposition completes the introductory material and introduces the body of the sermon by describing what is going to be discussed (i.e. the main points). For this reason, the preacher must work to move the introduction towards this final component in order to get the sermon off the ground. The following is an example of an introduction made for John 3:16 that incorporates the ideas presented so far in this chapter.

> *As a child I can remember having a well-populated list of things that I wanted to receive on Christmas morning or on my birthday. While I love to receive gifts, my wife loves to give gifts (and it is a good thing too as she has taken charge of making sure most our family and friends receive theirs on time!). Nothing puts a smile on her face more than someone opening a gift that she has carefully crafted*

or picked out for a special occasion. Gifts are fun to give and fun to receive and they ultimately reveal something of our love for one another. It is no different with God. Think of the many gifts He has given you. Your sustained life, a loving family, shelter, the seasons that we enjoy, something pretty to look at each sunrise and sunset, etc. However, today we are going to take a close look at three truths concerning God's greatest gift to mankind from one of the Bible's most popular verses, John 3:16. This gift, as does any present, tells us something about God's love and ultimately results in an important choice that every human being must make. Today, let us take a look at John 3:16 and witness three truths concerning the Love of God.

Conclusions

Everyone can think of someone who, when telling a story, never knows how to bring it to a close or get to the point. Instead, these story-tellers string an infinite regression of details or repetitive series of facts that never arrives anywhere. Unfortunately, the plane that took off at the beginning of the conversation never lands. This experience is similar to what congregations can expect when their preacher does not know how to successfully conclude his sermons. Therefore, just as special attention was necessary to build an introduction, so too must attention be given to the crafting of fine conclusions.

Characteristics

There are conclusions and there are good conclusions. Good conclusions are those conclusions that are united to the sermon. In other words, a conclusion does not begin a new topic or exist as a separate entity. Instead, it is neatly attached to the sermon body like a carefully constructed puzzle-piece that completes the whole picture. This requires planning. If the sermon is heading toward the conclusion, the conclusion must satisfy the congregation's ongoing curiosity concerning the destination they have been trying to reach for the past 25-30 minutes. Attention must be given so that this destination satisfies the expectations of the passage and the congregation. For this reason, as was recommended in the introduction, it is helpful for the preacher to write out his conclusion in the sermon-preparation process.

Clarity and coherence are other characteristics of good conclusions. The conclusion is where the preacher may answer potential questions concerning the implications of the passage that has just been preached. Similarly, the conclusion is the place to add clarity to the message and connect the message of the text to the context of the congregation. Because of the Bible's transcendent relevance, there are always opportunities to correctly apply God's Word in practical ways.[13] Therefore, it is up to the preacher to communicate the text's application for the audience appropriately.

Also, personal conclusions are good conclusions. Members of the congregation want to know that the preacher has personally wrestled with the text he is presenting. Anytime it is possible and appropriate, a preacher must demonstrate that he is working on applying the text in his life in the same way he is encouraging others to apply the text in their lives. By being personal in the conclusion, the pastor will develop a sense of camaraderie with the congregation and will find that it is easier to motivate change through what he has said in the sermon body. This will also help the preacher be more persuasive and forceful when he calls upon the congregation to commit in a specific area or make a decision.

---

[13] For a practical guide in reaching appropriate applications for passages consult Duvall & Hayes, *Grasping God's Word 2nd Ed.* (Grand Rapids, MI: Zondervan, 2005).

Construction

There are three important elements that the preacher needs to keep in mind when drafting a fitting conclusion to his sermon. First, it is paramount that the conclusion be in keeping with the aim and scope of the proposition of the sermon. Just as the body of the sermon was limited to the text and focused on the text by means of the sure-fire proposition, so must its conclusion be. If there is anything in the conclusion that does not fall under the umbrella of the proposition, it must be taken out.

In most cases it is appropriate to restate the proposition in the end of the sermon by way of summarizing what has been discussed. This helpful exercise will remind the audience what they have heard and keep the pastor on track.

> *"Repetition leads to retention"*
> -Dwayne Carson

Occam's razor (or cutting the fluff) and the K.I.S.S. principle (Keep It Simple Stupid) inform the next element of good conclusions— brevity. By their very nature, conclusions have an ending in sight and are designed to reach that ending as efficiently as possible. This is why the preacher must not use the conclusion to enter into a rabbit trail or travel along some new tangent. This is also why it should be kept simple. A preacher's ability to say what he needs to in the most concise way is an ability that must be cultivated. This is especially crucial at the end of the sermon when final remarks are given and applications are encouraged.

Finally, the conclusion needs to include the answer to one simple question, "So what?" People want to know what the big deal is concerning what has been said and immediately connect it in some way to their lives and experiences. If the congregation cannot walk away from a sermon knowing what to do in response to what they have heard, the preacher has failed. Instead, the pastor must take time in the conclusion to guide those he is preaching in the ways of applying the truths of God's Word practically. Conclusions that answer the so what question recognize the Bible as both a source of information and transformation.

Avoidances

Several different types of conclusions should be avoided by preachers at all times. One is the "touchdown conclusion." This type of conclusion is a conclusion that delivers something exciting and yet does not give resolution to the sermon. In other words the main question of the sermon is neglected altogether and a new issue is spiked in its place. Ultimately, the promise made by the preacher (to learn and apply a specific principle from a passage of Scripture) is broken. To avoid conclusions like this, the preacher must finish what he started in the introduction.

Another type of conclusion to avoid is the circling conclusion, otherwise known as the rambling conclusion. Everyone has experienced this type of conclusion before. They are the conclusions that leave congregations searching for the nearest exit and taking second glances at their watches, begging the preacher to "just get it over with." To prevent these conclusions, the preacher needs to be careful not to excessively repeat himself and work towards the end instead of getting lost in his thoughts or infatuated with the sound of his own voice.

A final conclusion that should be avoided is the detachable conclusion (a.k.a. the "caboose conclusion"). These are those sermon endings that are overly general and could be fixed to the end of just about any sermon. Like a caboose that can be detached from one train and attached to another, these conclusions do not play any significant role in the meaning or development of any one sermon. Care must be taken to customize each conclusion for each sermon so that every presentation of God's Word has its own appropriate ending.

With all of the characteristics and avoidances in mind, the following is a proposed conclusion for the sermon given on John 3:16.

> *God loves the world. His love is witnessed in His gift to the world. God's love results in eternal life for all who believe. When we understand the incredible love God has expressed for us in this life and the incredible act of love He bestowed toward the world, we are presented with two choices. Either we respond by placing our trust in Jesus Christ (God's most precious gift) and receive eternal life, or we deny the gift entirely and perish. If God so loves the world, that is the wicked whole of all that populates this sphere hurtling through space, then that means that He loves you, yes, even you. Not only does He love you, He loves you so much that He offers you His greatest gift, His Son Jesus Christ. Will you accept Him? Will you embrace God's best for your life? Or will you continue to settle for inferior love and the world's inferior presents? Know today that it is not too late in life for you to change directions, repent, and place your faith in Jesus Christ. This is the only way to know eternal life. Grow in your appreciation for what God has done in order for you to have real life. Show someone this week that you have this life by sharing God's greatest gift with others.*

Like bookends to a well-populated shelf of resources, the introduction and conclusion hold all of the content of the sermon together as one cohesive whole. Their undeniable importance cannot be overstated. These two elements introduce the truths of God's

Word and then apply the truths of God's Word in response to the presentation of God's Word. For these reasons, great care needs to be taken with these two elements for the glory of God and the benefit of the congregation.

PART II

The Art of Sermonizing

CHAPTER 4

Applying the Polish

"Whatever you do in word or deed, do all in the name of the Lord Jesus, giving thanks through Him to God the Father."
-Colossians 3:17

In high school, marching band was not just an extra-curricular activity; it was a way of life. Our 200-piece band was, at least in our minds, the real reason why people came to watch the football games. These feelings of significance drove us to hours of rehearsal each week where painstaking attention to detail fueled an ever-present pursuit of refinement. In the same way we would shine our horns, the band was always finding ways to buff out the rusty bits of our show in order to present a good product on Friday nights. We recognized that correct notes and forms on the field were not enough to get the fans on their feet following our final crescendo into the last note.

In much the same way, a good outline and accurate content are not enough to produce an exceptional sermon. There are certain practices that, if absent, will leave the preacher with a mechanical and awkward presentation. This chapter exists in an effort to polish up the sermon that this resource has been in the process of building and turn it into something truly remarkable and God-glorifying.

"It is time to put your preachin' shoes on!"

-Doc

Jeff Dickson

Transitions

If the points of an outline are the different forms (pictures a band creates on a marching field) of the sermon content, then transitions are the means the preacher uses to move from form to form. In fact, if transitions do not hold the sermon together, then the preacher runs the risk of presenting something that will fall apart in the minds of the listener. Transitional indicators demand that the audience listen and think more carefully as the sermon moves along. This is why special attention must be given in order to make sure that transitions show up in the sermonic presentation.

Transitions are necessary for several reasons. First, they provide clarity of thought. Understanding how one idea is connected to the previous idea mentioned allows progression and helps the big picture come into focus. One appreciates each picture that a marching band creates in their show in the same way each idea of a sermon contributes to the main points being given. This appreciation is cultivated if each idea is connected with effective transitions.

Transitions also create smoothness in a sermon as it develops from point to point. Without them, the sermon inevitably seems fragmented or disconnected. This would be like a marching band standing in one form and then awkwardly moving to the next form without any uniformity.

Finally, transitions help the sermon become more efficient. In other words, transitions move the sermon along toward the conclusion. This keeps the audience from getting tired or bored by what is being said, as they can feel the progression toward the sermon's natural end.

Good transitions are "transporters." This means that they carry the audience into the next part of the sermon. In many ways, the relationship between the preacher and his congregation is like that of a marching band director and his/her students. The director guides the students along to each part of the marching show and takes time to explain how it fits together in order that everyone understands what is going on at all times. The director never assumes that his students know where they are going next and neither should the preacher. Instead, the preacher should make it as easy for his congregation to follow him and never neglect being helpful along the way. The moment a preacher assumes his audience is already privy to where he is heading is the moment he runs the risk of losing his audience.

Another characteristic of good transitions is that they should be varied. No one wants to hear the same transition at every turn of the sermon in the same way no one wants to hear the same musical phrase over and over again accompanied by the same routine when they watch a marching performance. Therefore, the preacher must become skilled at providing variety in the way he connects the sermon together. Below are some suggestions of different types of transitions one might choose to use.

1. Numbers: "first, second, third, etc."
2. Summaries: "we have already discussed . . . Now, we are going to . . ."
3. Bridge words: "again, in addition, besides, moreover, another thing, on the other hand, finally, etc."
4. Illustrations: "In many ways, this principle is like . . ."

Good transitions are also planned. This is especially important when the preacher moves from one major point to the next major point of his sermon. In these instances, the preacher must plan carefully so that the audience knows without a shadow of a doubt that the sermon is moving to its next major division. Just as a marching band does not magically transition from form to form on a whim, transitions like these do not happen by accident.

> *"Proper Planning Prevents Poor Performance"*
>
> -Doc

Planned transitions result in an audience that knows exactly where they are in the midst of a sermon. In the John 3:16 example already presented, if the preacher wanted to successfully move from the first to the second point, he might say something like, "Now that we understand the first truth of this passage, it is important that we move onto the second major truth of this passage, 'God's love is witnessed in His gift.'"

One helpful measure in preparing good transitions includes writing them out in the sermon planning process. If transitions are written out, then they can be rehearsed, memorized, and put into practice during the sermon. It is also helpful to accompany transitions with a pause in the sermon presentation. Often, pauses will alert the audience that something new or important is about to be shared (such as the next major point or the conclusion). A preacher may also decide to inflect his voice in a different way in order to make a clear transition. This is useful when a preacher moves from an illustration to the main sermon content or uses a more reflective tone in an invitation. Another way a good preacher transitions is through his body language. Moving back behind the pulpit may be a way to suggest that the sermon is moving on to the next point. Similarly, moving down off the platform may suggest that the sermon is nearing its end.

If any preacher desires to move from good to great for the glory of God, he must not neglect the polish that good transitions can provide. They are paramount to the overall effect, fluidity, movement, and cohesiveness of the sermon. However, this is not the only way to shine up one's presentation of God's Word.

Illustrations

Although the musical nuances and drill design of a marching band performance help convey the overall meaning of the show, the color guard is another important piece of the presentation that works to illustrate what is going on in the music. Flag colors along with costumes accentuate the performance and help reveal the meaning of the music in terms that the audience can appreciate and understand. The more appropriately the color guard is applied to a marching band performance, the more the audience walks away with an understanding of what the presentation was all about. The same might be said of illustrations in a sermon.

An illustration is an analogy that explains or applies truth. Normally, these are concrete examples used to support general assertions, thereby reducing the level of abstraction for the congregation.

> *"Illustrations are the window which lets in the light of understanding to that which is unknown"*
>
> -Doc

In sermonic presentation, illustrations are creative ways to aid the audience's understanding and application of God's Word. They grab the attention of the congregation, focus on the Word of God, and demand a response. For these reasons, illustrations are helpful additions to any sermon as they add shine to its overall effect.

Unfortunately, illustrations can be a dangerous mine-field in the practice of preaching. Many of today's preachers fail to understand what good illustrations look like and misuse them altogether. Often, a misplaced illustration or unfortunate analogy can come across like a dropped flag on the football field, stealing focus away from the show. Therefore it is important to distinguish the difference between a good illustration and a bad illustration.

First, good illustrations are fresh and interesting. These types of illustrations often come from life experiences and personal observations. People, whether they want to admit it or not, are interested in the life of the preacher. Therefore, opportunities to share from personal experiences should be taken when appropriate.

Similarly, the congregation is often interested in how the preacher views the world. This means that the pastor should share his observations at the right place and the right time in the sermon.

Illustrations of this kind need to focus on the preacher and not on other members of the congregation. Preachers need to be careful not to hurt anybody else's feelings by pointing unnecessary attention to individuals or ever exposing a confidence. This is important with family or close friends. A preacher should refrain from always using his family or personal friends in his sermon illustrations, especially without their permission. This will help protect from annoyance or embarrassment.

Not only are good illustrations fresh, they are convincing. If a preacher desires to illustrate a point, he must be sure to avoid errors of fact. If a church member chooses to investigate the legitimacy of an illustration (that is presented as legitimate), they need to be able to discover that everything checks out fine. In order to prevent errors like these, the preacher must be careful not to put himself in illustrations that did not actually happen to him (i.e. lying). If a preacher wants to share someone else's experience, he needs to give the source of that experience instead of claiming it for himself. Another way to solve this problem would be to present a story as just that, a story.

Good illustrations should also illustrate something about the sermon. Too often preachers begin a long diatribe or personal story that has little or no relationship to the text with which they are dealing. At best, these are "fluff," and, at worst, these are red-herrings that distract people from the Word of God. Therefore, attention must be given to demonstrate how each inserted illustration naturally supports what the Bible is trying to communicate or how it applies to the congregation.

Another characteristic of a good illustration is understandability. An analogy or anecdote is not going to do the sermon any good if no one can comprehend what it is about. Arriving at understandable illustrations involves understanding the audience. If the preacher is preaching in Europe, he needs to leave uniquely American illustrations out of the sermon, lest he confuse his audience. Similarly, if the preacher is speaking to children, he needs make sure his illustrations are kid-friendly and easier to comprehend. Knowing what the audience is capable of understanding and appreciating will help the preacher choose proper illustrations.

Here are some other helpful reminders.

1. Avoid details that clutter the story.
2. Visualize your illustration before you give it.
3. Plan illustrations in advance.
4. Draw from your everyday life.
5. Watch nonverbal cues from the audience as you give your illustrations.

Good illustrations have the potential of serving all kinds of meaningful purposes in the sermon. Below is a list of just some of the ways illustrations can be utilized by the preacher.

Illustrations can

1. Illuminate the subject
2. Obtain and hold interest
3. Galvanize creativity
4. Establish rapport with the audience
5. Rest the audience
6. Clarify the subject
7. Make truth vivid
8. Strengthen an argument
9. Bring conviction of sin
10. Persuade
11. Aid the memory
12. Ornament the sermon

13. Inject touches of humor
14. Stimulate hearer's imagination
15. Speak to difficult situations indirectly
16. Appeal to children
17. Make a message practical

This list demonstrates the wide range of possibilities illustrations have and the copious ways in which a preacher can present the principles of the text.

An equally compelling list might be the various types of illustrations that preachers may choose to use. Here are just a few to keep in mind when preparing a sermon.

1. Stories
2. Object lessons
3. Reenacting a scene
4. Allegories (sustained or prolonged metaphors)
5. Figurative language
6. Poems
7. Analogies
8. Quotations
9. Statistics
10. Current Events
11. Videos
12. Pictures

Illustrations like these and many others can be discovered in the Bible itself, personal experiences and observations, nature, athletics, media, biographies, historical accounts, literature, science, art, archaeology, contemporary theology, and one's own imagination.

Ultimately, all of these different types of illustrations can be divided into two categories. First, there are those that are explanatory. In the sermon manuscript of John 3:16 given earlier, the illustration of the word "love" and the difference between my love for Dr. Pepper and my love for my wife worked to explain the uniqueness of God's love for the world. A good preacher will use illustrations like these when dealing with abstract concepts or complex issues in the Bible.

There are also applicational illustrations. These illustrations work to apply a biblical truth to a specific scenario, whether fictional or realistic. An example of this would be the hypothetical situation of the congregation giving their prized possession to a sworn enemy in an effort to illustrate the gift of God's only begotten Son. In this illustration, God's activity was applied to a potential scenario for every listener to consider hypothetically. Illustrations like these are especially useful in the conclusion of the sermon when the preacher is calling the congregation to action.

Creativity

In each successive marching season, it always seemed like we were innovating further and further in the area of creativity and thinking outside of the box in order to stay competitive with other high school bands. Marching and playing were no longer enough in order to stay on the cutting edge and remain current with the best groups. This is why visuals, voice-overs, solos, and even dancing became a part of the shows we would perform. Ultimately, in order to become great, we had to be creative. The same is true of great sermons.

Consider for a moment the creativity of God Himself. He is the same God who colored the cloud nebulae, spotted the giraffe, and designed the Himalayan Mountains! Having been made in His image, we too are creative and have been given creativity as one of the ways to glorify Him. Creativity is the ability to express relationships in a new or different way. It answers the question, "How else can I say this?" Therefore, preachers must determine to put this ability to good use in their sermons in order to present God's truth in a fresh and God-glorifying way.

The importance of creativity cannot be understated. It has the potential of infecting a sermon with a quality of enthusiasm and keeps it from being cold or dry. Creativity also increases the quality of the presentation and ensures the effectiveness of a preacher's communicative ability. In other words, creative preachers are those who are able to say what others have said in a way that no one else has said it. These are the sermons that preachers will discover are worth sharing and the homilies that congregations will discover are worth remembering.

Although some might be more naturally creative than others, creativity is something that any preacher can cultivate in his repertoire. The first way of cultivating creativity is to get preaching experience.

> *"The best way to learn how to preach*
> *is to do it as often as you can"*
>
> -Doc

Preaching experience will invite growth in the area of creativity and allow the preacher to look back on what he has presented and ask himself, "How can I say this differently the next time I give this sermon?"

One other way of igniting creativity in one's preaching is to develop outside interests or hobbies. The marching band illustration in this chapter is a creative element that is a reflection of an outside interest that I continue to have to this day. In fact, this chapter would be severely lacking in creativity without my outside interest in marching bands. People can discover creative elements from just about anywhere: life experiences, taste in music or theatre, sports, etc. Preachers need to use these outside interests to their advantage and get creative in their exposition of the Creator.

Wise preachers would benefit from observing what creative preachers do in their sermons. Observing the response of the congregation is also helpful. If people in the pews seem alert and are taking notes then the preacher might be doing a good job of preaching in a creative way. However, if they are nodding off or looking around, then the preacher may need to spice things up. Recording and listening to past sermons may also reveal what is lacking in the area of creativity. When a preacher nods off to his own sermon, he knows he needs to improve his presentation of God's Word.

Creativity shows up in the different illustrations a preacher decides to use and the types of sermons he commits to preach. Though every sermon should be a sermon (i.e. preaching in its truest sense as described before), a preacher may decide to preach a verse sermon instead of a passage sermon every now and then or intersperse a topical sermon when appropriate. This kind of variety will develop creativity and prove refreshing to any audience.

The preacher needs to remember that these helpful items exist for the text and not for his own prestige. Anything that becomes so bold that it steals focus from the Word of God has no place in any sermon. The text and its communication must reign supreme at all times. With this in mind, transitions, illustrations, and general creativity can work together to make a sermon shine and will result in a presentation that is both aesthetically pleasing to the audience and glorifying to God.

CHAPTER 5

Avoiding the Pitfalls

"The prudent sees danger and hides himself,
but the simple go on and suffer for it."
-Proverbs 22:3

I frequently walk the neighborhood that surrounds my church in order to meet people and pray for the community. Time spent in reflection and quiet meditation on the Lord is accentuated in these walks by the beautiful Virginia weather and stillness of the midday. Often, it seems as though God and I are the only ones out and that we have the entire neighborhood to ourselves. However, nearly every time I go on one of these walks, I trip on those parts of the sidewalk that have split and shifted over the years. Every time I stub my toe my communion with the Lord is briefly interrupted by frustration and pain! Needless to say, these cracks in the concrete have become pitfalls to avoid whenever I take these treasured prayer walks.

As preachers develop in their ability to present God's Word, there are several pitfalls that they must avoid so that they do not trip themselves or their audience. This chapter will expose these obstacles and point the way around them. Those who look out for these pitfalls will be more equipped to lead their congregations in an uninterrupted journey through God's revelation.

Failing to Plan

One of the most common pitfalls of preachers today is a failure to plan. Those who learn the value of planning the hard way agree with the old adage, "failure to plan is planning to fail." This could not be more true for proclaiming the Word of God. In fact, if any task deserved a heightened level of planning, it is preaching. Although this resource has already aided the preacher in planning individual sermons, planning on a broader scale also needs to be addressed.

"Sunday is always, at most, six days away."

-Doc

Preachers often fail to remember that the countdown to the next Sunday begins immediately after the invitation is complete. Those who are surprised by their next preaching engagement are failing to plan properly. This is why a preaching calendar is helpful. A preaching calendar is a long range planning program applied to the task of preaching. This organizational tool is one way to avoid asking the embarrassing question, "What am I going to preach on next week?" Such a calendar alleviates last minute frustration and keeps the preacher from scrambling to put a message together on Saturday night.

Putting together a preaching calendar is relatively simple. First, the preacher must be sensitive to the needs of the people. Understanding where the congregation is geographically, spiritually, socio-economically, etc. will help the preacher establish a plan that is customized to his context. The Church year, holidays, special community events, and seasons should also be included in the planning process. Preaching calendars that take all of these things into consideration will naturally cultivate variety throughout the year and provide a natural progression of material that makes logical sense.

Another item to consider when putting a preaching calendar together is the readiness of the speaker. Preachers need to make a humble assessment of themselves by asking questions like, "What books do I have a firm grasp on?" and, "What topics am I familiar with?" Those books that are unfamiliar or beyond the preacher's grasp may need to be avoided until greater comprehension is achieved.

> **"You cannot lead anyone anywhere**
> **you have not already been."**
>
> -Doc

Preachers need to preach their strengths while working privately to alleviate their areas of weakness.

Preparing a preaching calendar should also involve dependency on the Holy Spirit. For too long, many have limited their understanding of the Holy Spirit's involvement to what is sporadic, spontaneous, and showy. This is a gross misinterpretation of who the Holy Spirit is. God is a God of order[14] and God has always been active in planning ahead. Therefore, the Holy Spirit can be just as active in planning a preaching calendar as He is when each sermon is given. In fact, the indwelling Holy Spirit of God is the agent behind anything of eternal significance that takes place in the life of a believer. If a preacher desires to plan a preaching schedule that results in change that will be experienced for eternity, he must submit himself entirely to the Holy Spirit's leadership in this preparatory step.

> **"But when He, the Spirit of truth, comes, He will**
> **guide you into all the truth; for He will not speak on**
> **His own initiative, but whatever He hears, He will**
> **speak; and He will disclose to you what is to come."**
>
> -John 16:13

---

[14] 1 Cor. 14:33.

> *"You will be surprised how many times a message that*
> *was planned months ago will meet a specific need, or*
> *speak to an immediate issue on the Sunday it is given"*
>
> -Doc

The natural outgrowth of a preaching calendar is a preaching reservoir. A preaching reservoir is the implementation of the long range preaching program expressed in the preaching calendar. Once a preacher knows what he is going to preach, he can prepare in advance by focusing his efforts to study those things that are coming up on the preaching calendar. Elements of his study that are included in the preaching reservoir are grammatical analysis, research, outline, and commentary. Preachers who are committed to building a preaching reservoir ahead of time will never be short of material to preach.

For instance, if a preacher decided to spend the better part of two years preaching through the book of John, the preaching calendar should reflect that on Sunday mornings, each service will cover the next passage of the fourth gospel (with the exception of special Sundays or seasonal messages). Knowing this, the preacher should spend the majority of his study time reading John (the first step), performing grammatical analysis on John (the second step), building an outline of John (the third step), and developing his own personal commentary on John (the fourth step). If this work is accomplished before the series begins, all the preacher has to do to prepare for each week in the series is extract a manageable passage from his commentary and convert it into a sermon by following the steps previously discussed. In essence, his commentary becomes his sermonic outline. The only thing left to do is to add an introduction, a conclusion, and polish.

Preaching reservoirs and preaching calendars allow for maturity and depth in preaching while building a preacher's repertoire for the future. If these methods are followed, those who preach through a book of the Bible end up with a commentary on that book that they can use and draw from for the rest of their lives.

Busy schedules, unforeseen circumstances, congregational demands, and copious responsibilities of preachers require that they do all that they can to help themselves. Planning by means of a preaching calendar and a preaching reservoir are two ways preachers can help themselves prepare for their greatest responsibility.

Losing your Balance

One of the elements involved in tripping or falling is losing one's balance. When equilibrium is interrupted for whatever reason, anyone is capable of taking a bad fall. The same is true of sermonic presentation. Unbalanced sermons can leave the congregation in a state of fallen interest or loss of understanding. This is why losing balance is an important pitfall to avoid.

A balanced sermon is a sermon that gives appropriate amounts of time to each of its important components. These parts include the introduction, body, and conclusion. A helpful rule to remember in order to establish how long each of these parts should run is the 10-80-10 principle. This rule states that around 10 percent of the sermon should be devoted to the introduction and 10 percent to the conclusion while 80 percent of the sermon should be devoted to the body. Below is a pictorial guide for this rule.

10% Intro.	80% Body	10% Concl.

"You wouldn't want to build a house with too big
a front porch or an unusually large back deck"

-Doc

It is important that the sermon get rolling at the beginning and wrap up in the end. If an introduction is too long, the congregation will begin to wonder if the sermon is ever going to start. Similarly, if one continues to ramble in the conclusion, the congregation will wonder if it is ever going to end. Therefore, this rule is a helpful way to avoid the pitfall of losing one's balance.

However, the 10-80-10 principle may have some exceptions. For instance, if a passage has a particularly important context, a longer introduction may be necessary in order to prepare the audience for what they are going to hear and how they should interpret what is being said. Also, passages that naturally lend themselves to important applications may need a longer conclusion so that the audience understands how to practice the principles they have learned in the body. Therefore, the lines drawn by the 10-80-10 principles are more like guidelines than strict demarcations.

Growing too Comfortable

Comfort is not hard to come by on my walks around South Roanoke. In fact, so pleasant and familiar are my surroundings that I often will forget that I need to watch out for obstacles in my way or bumps along the concrete sidewalk. Stubbed toes and embarrassing situations remind me all of the time that growing too comfortable is a pitfall worth avoiding. One of the very real dangers of preaching, and ministry in general, is growing too comfortable.

Variety is the antidote for growing too comfortable in one's preaching. If preachers preach the same type of sermon week after week, they will avoid the other ways God's Word can be presented. On the receiving end, congregations will begin to expect the same thing every week and lose interest in the way God's Word is being communicated. Variety keeps the preacher fresh and the congregation excited about what is being said. If Jesus taught in an assortment of ways (parables, miracles, anecdotes, biblical quotations, etc.), should not God's preachers adopt the same spirit of diversity?

The easiest way of cultivating variety is preaching different kinds of sermons. For instance, if the preacher is preaching through the book of John and predominately uses passage sermons, he might decide to cultivate variety by interspersing a verse sermon every now and then (especially on significant verses like John 3:16). Another way might be to take a verse that seems to address an important topic and preach that verse topically (such as John 11:25 and the resurrection). There are all kinds of possibilities for variety in sermonic presentation. However, with these different possibilities come great responsibilities.

Passage Sermon

There are many advantages to preaching passage sermons. For starters, passage sermons enable the preacher to deal with a complete unit of thought in one service. This type of sermon also allows the preacher to preach through a book faster and more efficiently. Passage sermons help the audience grasp the movement that is uncovered within the passages themselves as well as anticipate what is coming up. For all of these reasons and more, passage sermons are an efficient way to preach God's Word.

However, there are several things to keep in mind when using this type of presentation. First, preachers must understand that passage sermons tend to become too involved. Members of a congregation should only be expected to sit and give their attention for so long. Similarly, church members should only be expected to take in so much information. Preachers who love to preach passages need to be careful that their sermons not come off like shotgun blasts, peppering the people with loads of fragmented bits of facts. Preachers also need to be aware of the very real tendency passage sermons have of becoming a running commentary.

Because of their many advantages, passage sermons are normally the most common way of proclaiming God's Word (that is among those who are actually preaching in its truest sense). However these warnings remind expository preachers that even this efficient style of preaching has its own negative tendencies to evade. For a sample sermon manuscript of a passage sermon, see Appendix 4.

Verse Sermon

If a preacher is seeking variety, he might interrupt his flow of passages by focusing on a specific verse. Verse sermons are valuable because they display the vast richness of the Word of God by focusing the attention of the congregation on the fine points of meaning within a single Scripture unit. This type of sermon is especially helpful when a preacher comes across a difficult passage or doctrine. Verse sermons are able to dig deep into such verses and supply the congregation with solid spiritual nourishment. Digging deep in this way also pushes the preacher to perform serious study on individual units of God's Word.

Just like passage sermons, verse sermons have their own set of warnings. For many congregations, verse sermons tend to become monotonous if they are used too often. Similarly, they tend to become tedious as they can labor over small and sometimes insignificant points. Preachers who love verse sermons often make a big deal out of nothing and over-emphasize minutia. Overuse of verse sermons can also keep people from maintaining a firm grasp of the book as a whole as they tend to ride hobby-horses and are easily taken out of context. Although effective for certain verses, verse sermons need to be used sparingly and carefully. An example of a verse sermon can be found earlier in this resource for John 3:16.

Topical Sermon

Another alternative to preaching passage sermons is preaching a topical sermon. A topical sermon takes a passage or verse that deals with a specific topic or doctrine and teaches that topic or doctrine from the lense of that verse or passage along with the aid of other Scriptures that speak to the subject at hand. This type of sermon allows the preacher to deal with a subject logically and enables the congregation to see the rational development of a particular subject. Topical sermons help demonstrate how subjects relate to each other in the Word of God and they enable the preacher to deal with doctrines in a systematic way. These are a good way to instruct the congregation theologically or tie together several books that have been previously preached.

However, topical sermons are abused everywhere all the time. Preachers who desire to really preach must heed the warnings associated with this style of preaching. First, topical sermons tend to circle around a preacher's wheel-house to an unhealthy extent. If a pastor loves to talk about the family, he will preach the topic of family into everything he can find. If another enjoys educating people about money, finance will occupy the majority of his sermons.

The real danger of this is discovered when preachers like these begin to handle the Scripture deductively (from the outside in or from experience to revelation) instead of inductively (from the inside out or from revelation to experience). Overuse of the topical preaching method can also leave the preacher open to taking verses out of context and coming up with a topic on the spot without consulting the Scriptures at all. Therefore, topical sermons should supplement a preaching schedule and not be overused. Please consult Appendix 5 for an example manuscript of a topical sermon.

Variety is essential and comfort is dangerous. Preachers should be constantly challenging themselves to find opportunities to keep their congregation on the edge of their seat and interested in the Word of God. This is why these different preaching styles should be used at the appropriate time and in the appropriate way.

Becoming a Distraction

Like a stubbed toe during a prayer walk, distractions are an impending threat to any sermon. They steal people's attention and rob the sermon of focus. Although preachers cannot control everything around them at all times, one thing they can control is becoming a distraction to their own sermon. Below is a small glossary of bad habits that preachers are often unaware of that distract the congregation from what is being said. Though they may seem petty, anything that steals attention from God's Word rather than accentuates it is a big problem.

Weight-Shifting (Why is he swaying?)

This describes the phenomenon of swaying back and forth. This is a nervous habit that makes the preacher look like he is riding a ship on troubled waters. Many preachers who constantly move in this way are unaware that they are even doing it. If a preacher decides to remain in one place for an extended period of time, he should take care not to constantly sway, lest the congregation notice the continual pendulum swing and get sea sick!

Aimless Wandering (Where is he going?)

Many who move while preaching do so with purpose, adding to the sermonic flow of the presentation. However, there are those who pace back and forth or wander aimlessly. Movement that is unmotivated can become a distraction to the sermon. Also, constantly pacing back and forth can wear your congregation out.

Unusual Gesturing (What is he doing?)

There are as many unique gestures as there are preachers. While certain hand movements or other forms of body language add flavor and uniqueness to a sermon, others are unusual enough to become a distraction. Here are just a few worth mentioning.

The Bear Claw-For whatever reason, many preachers love to make contact with the pulpit with their hands. However, clawing at the top of pulpit is a gesture that, more often than not, does not relate to what is being said in any meaningful way. This gesture almost appears as though the preacher is raking leaves toward the bottom lip of the podium. This can become a distraction among the congregation.

The Holy Triangle-The Holy triangle is the gesture formed when the hands come together in front of the pastor with the fingers pointing down and the thumbs pointed upward (forming what appears to be a triangle in the center). This gesture is a weak stance and is often a neutral pose that "high church" clergy use. Though not wrong or inappropriate, this gesture can become debilitating. Many subconsciously use this gesture to the neglect of other more useful gestures.

The Tripod-This is the gesture formed when preachers grip each end of the pulpit with their hands. This gesture is ill-advised because it closes the preacher off from his congregation, brings the preacher's head down, and makes the preacher look like he is nervous.

The Windmill-Twirling one's arms around in a circular motion is highly useful if one is directing traffic, hoping someone will hurry, or, even in a sermon trying to communicate something that is ongoing or repetitive. However, twirling one's arms (especially both of them), is not a gesture that one should incorporate all of the time. This gesture is tiring for both the preacher and the audience watching.

The Lounger—It is important that the preacher look comfortable and relaxed during the sermon. However, while it is permissible for the hands to be in the pockets, they should not remain there for very long. Such a pose does nothing to help the preacher and can only hurt or distract.

A couple of helpful ways to alleviate these and any other distracting gestures from one's presentation is to ask the question, "What does this gesture mean?" or "What motivates this movement?" Doing something out of habit, because it feels good, or because the preacher has always done it is not a justifiable reason to leave it in the sermon. Gestures should add to what is being said in a meaningful way and not distract the listener from the sermon content.

Awkward Staring (Who is he looking at?)

Preachers also unknowingly distract their audiences by staring. Staring can occur at multiple levels. One is toward the pulpit. If a preacher disengages his audience by staring at his Bible or sermon notes, the audience will disengage from the sermon.

Another way staring is manifested is when preachers decide to continually look at a specific area of the sanctuary, group of people in the room or, heaven forbid, an individual. Staring like this will make the audience wonder, "What is he looking at?" or "Who is he speaking to?"

Finally, staring into space should also be avoided. This happens because of nerves or because the pastor is more wrapped up in his own mind than in what is being said to the people. Staring like this may leave people wondering, "Is he searching for his next thought?" or "Is he looking for some kind of inspiration?" All of these staring problems should be avoided at all costs.

Meaningless Murmuring (Why does he keep saying . . . ?)

Words are precious to every sermon as each one purposefully transports the truth of God's Word from the page to the congregation. Therefore, those words that do not aid this process should be taken out. These include vocalized pauses like "uh" or "um," fillers like "like," "okay," or "all right," and repetitive phrases such as "you know," or "the fact of the matter is." Words and phrases like this are fluff and contribute nothing to what is preached. In fact, members of the congregation may even take up the task of charting exactly how many times the preacher repeats any number of these phrases for fun! (I speak from experience here.)

Preachers hoping to avoid these kinds of distractions should humble themselves by watching video footage of past sermons they have given. This exercise will expose habits and illuminate certain behaviors that the preacher may not even be aware of. Once a preacher identifies how he might be distracting his people, he can learn how to alleviate it in the future.

> *"Each week there are at least five different sermons that are preached. There is the sermon on the page of your notes, the sermon that you think you give, the sermon that you actually give, the sermon that the congregation hears, and the sermon that they apply."*
>
> -Doc

No preacher is perfect. However, good preachers are those who are aware of the pitfalls that can keep their sermons from having the maximum impact on their congregations for the glory of God. It is vitally important for preachers to plan ahead, keep their balance, cultivate variety, and alleviate distractions in order that they do not stub their toe in front of everyone or trip their congregation while on the path to biblical truth.

Addressing the art of presentation is important if any preacher wants to do his best in the sacred task of preaching God's Word. Applying the polish and avoiding the pitfalls will result in people confronting God's truth in the best possible way and applying its principles properly. However, the art of presentation is to be used for the benefit of the message, not the messenger. If people are enamored, let them be enamored by the glory of God as demonstrated in His Word.

PART III

The Miracle of Voicing

CHAPTER 6

Investigating the Instrument

*"I will give thanks to You, for I am
fearfully and wonderfully made;
Wonderful are Your works,
And my soul knows it very well."*

-Psalm 139:14

One Sunday at the church I currently serve, a high-profile minister visited and proved to be an intimidating presence in the service (especially for me as a brand new preacher!). Though I would like to pretend his being there had no effect on my preaching, nothing could have been further from the truth. After the sermon was complete and the invitation accomplished, I asked if this visiting minister would dismiss our congregation in prayer. As he opened his mouth, I could not help but admire the rich smooth voice God had given him and imagine what he must have sounded like when he preached in his prime. This tranquil feeling of admiration soon turned into jealousy as I have not been gifted with the deep and soothing voice that our congregation enjoyed for those few moments. My wife even commented after the service that she could have listened to that voice all day long!

Though some voices might be more aesthetically pleasing than others, all are unique and useful for proclaiming the gospel when understood and used properly.

> **"You are the only one that has ever
> had or will have your voice"**
>
> -Doc

Like a fingerprint, a voice is one marker that God has given every individual that sets them apart from everyone else. This is no different for preachers.

Learning what to say and how to present it are two fundamental principles of preaching that this resource has already investigated. However, many preachers and the resources designed for them do not address the voice itself and the many intricacies that surround the phenomenon of speaking. How does the voice work? Should all preachers sound alike? Why is it important that a preacher obtain their optimum pitch and use their voice properly for preaching? These and other questions will be answered in these final two chapters.

The Anatomy of the Voice

The best musicians in the world are those who understand their instruments the most. Similarly, those preachers who understand the incredible instrument God has given them will be able to use it in the best possible way for His glory. What follows is a short biology lesson that identifies and explains the major parts of the anatomy required for vocalizing.

Cricoid Cartilage

Moving from the bottom of the larynx (or voice box) up, the first part of the vocal anatomy pertinent for this discussion is the cricoid cartilage. Sitting on top of the trachea (commonly known as the wind pipe), the cricoid cartilage provides the foundation for the larynx and all subsequent voicing cartilages. All of the air moving in or out of the lungs is either inspired or expired through the opening formed by this circular cartilage that is roughly the size of a man's wedding ring!

Arytenoid Cartilage

Sitting directly on top of the cricoid cartilage and attached to this ring is the arytenoid cartilage. This mirrored cartilage rotates to open and close the vocal folds (vocal cords). During normal breathing, the arytenoid cartilage is arranged in an open formation to allow the free passage of air. During voicing, the arytenoid cartilage is held in a closing pattern to allow the vibration of the vocal folds to create speech as the air moves past.

Thyroid Cartilage

The next major element of the larynx that is significant to voicing is the thyroid cartilage. The thyroid cartilage is a paired lamina cartilage. In men the lamina are joined at a 90° angle and in women at a 130° angle. The thyroid cartilage's main purpose is to house the vocal folds which run from the front of the thyroid cartilage to the arytenoid cartilages posteriorily. Men have a protruding thyroid cartilage which forms what many refer to as an "Adam's apple." Because the dramatic angle stretches the vocal folds across a longer barrier, the voice is deeper (much as longer strings on a piano achieve lower notes). A woman's thyroid cartilage is not nearly as angled and because of its lesser protrusion creates a higher voice (because the vocal folds are stretched over a shorter distance).

Vocal Folds

Commonly known as the vocal cords or vocalis, the vocal folds are the source of voicing. When closed by the arytenoid cartilages, the vocal folds vibrate as air is expelled from the lungs and form a buzzing that reverberates in the throat, sinuses, and mouth. This noise, after it bounces off the throat, curvature of the tongue, and the shape of the lips against the teeth, creates speech. In fact, if you were to hear the sound created by the vocal folds before it hits anything beyond it, it would be similar to the noise heard by a trumpet player when he or she buzzes into his or her mouthpiece. Attractive sound is only achieved by a trumpeter when the buzzing mouthpiece is attached to the series of curves and valves of the rest of the instrument. Similarly, voicing is attractive because the buzzing sound created by the vocal folds passes through the throat, sinuses, and mouth before it is heard.

Epiglottis Cartilage

The upper end of the larynx is open, and the area just above the vocal folds is known as the glottis. The epiglottis cartilage opens and closes depending on what activity is performed. When someone swallows food or drink the epiglottis covers the glottis and diverts the food into the esophagus, keeping it from entering the larynx. When breathing or voicing is taking place, the glottis is open so that air may move freely in and out of the lungs. Choking occurs when food somehow passes through the glottis and inhibits the passage of air through the larynx. When this happens, coughing is the body's way of clearing the larynx to allow proper air flow. In extreme cases, the Heimlich maneuver is used to force food out of the cricoid opening in order to reestablish breathing.

Although a hyoid bone and other minor structures are seen in various diagrams of the larynx, the cartilages described above are those which are essential for speech and necessary to include in this discussion on the miracle of voicing.

The Voicing Phenomenon

Now that God's design of the human voice has been appreciated, how He decided to accomplish speech will be explained in detail so that preachers may achieve speech in the best possible way and return glory to Him by serving His people. A pipe organ is impressive in form and function. However, it can only be fully appreciated when air is moving through the structure as it is played. Similarly, a voice's structure and form is remarkable. However, voices are enjoyed most when air is used to create speech.

Up until the mid-20th century, little was understood about the phenomenon of speech. Cadavers provided little help in understanding how people were able to speak and experiments on live individuals were thought impossible. However, courageous scientists like Thomas J. Hixon soon revolutionized this scientific field and provided answers to the looming questions surrounding our ability to communicate vocally.

Zealous in his pursuit of solving the mystery of voicing, Hixon took to performing experiments on himself. After inserting a series of balloons in his throat on separate occasions along with the use of precariously placed needles in his thyroid, Hixon was able to solve the mystery of voicing for the entire world. He learned that normal breathing was a result of air being drawn into the lungs and expelled from the lungs when the vocal folds were open, allowing air to move uninhibited through the cricoid cartilage above the trachea.[15] However, he determined that voicing was much more involved.

---

[15] Thomas J. Hixon & Collaborators, *Respiratory Function in Speech and Song* (Boston, MS: College Hill, 1987), 7-17.

Preparing for Speech

Simple or involuntary breathing does not require much air in the lungs at any one time. Because of this, taking in air while the body is at rest results in the chest expanding and contracting because of the air moving in and out of the lungs. However, speech or singing requires more air. This is why the diaphragm is important. Sitting beneath the lungs, the diaphragm is a muscle that allows for deeper breathing by pushing the abdominal organs down and drawing more air into the respiratory system. When anyone breathes after enlisting the help of their diaphragm, the stomach expands because more air is moving into the lungs and pushing the abdomen down.

This larger amount of air allows for a stronger voice and longer periods of speech without taking breaths. In fact, preachers who suffer from a shallow voice or multiple breaths in a short amount of time are probably guilty of insufficient breathing. In order to correct this, preachers must cultivate the use of the diaphragm in order to draw in more air and achieve a better, longer-lasting voice while speaking. To make sure you are breathing properly, think about pushing your stomach out instead of making your chest as big as possible. This will naturally result in greater inspiration of air.

Exercise

In order to check and see if you are breathing properly for sermonizing, try the chair test. This involves sitting up in any ordinary hard seat with your back firmly against the chair. If you can feel the lower portion of your back gently grazing the chair when air is taken in, then it is clear that the diaphragm is being used properly to take in the maximum amount of air possible. Preachers who breathe this way will not have to take in as many breaths during the sermon and will inevitably have greater vocal quality.

Performing Speech

After the air has been taken in, speech can occur. Though some scientists prior to the mid-20th century speculated that the brain sent messages to the muscles in the throat in order to create speech, Hixon and others discovered that the throat muscles play only a small role in the speaking process. The subtle movements of the arytenoid cartilage to close the vocal folds and the opening of the epiglottis are really the only two active movements that the throat makes during speech.

Though there may not be many muscles activated to create the movement necessary for speech, the air that is expelled out of the lungs during speech vibrates the vocal folds in order to produce sound in a passive way. This sound is then bounced off other areas of the throat and mouth to produce various speech acts.

While speech is taking place, the lungs contract as the air moves out and the diaphragm moves into a checking pattern. Contrary to popular belief, the diaphragm does not push air out of the body; it is only used to draw air into the body. Instead, other muscle groups that surround the torso fulfill this purpose. The different muscle groups used to squeeze air out of the body during speech depend on the duration of the speech act that takes place in between breaths.

Once air begins to flow out of the lungs during speech and the diaphragm moves into the checking position (back to neutral), the external intercostal muscles begin to flex. These muscles line the outside of the rib cage and help squeeze air out of the lungs during speech. As time continues without another breath, the body then uses its internal intercostal muscles to help push more air out of the lungs. Lining the inside of the rib-cage, these muscles almost mirror the external intercostal muscles in form and function.

If breathing does not take place and speech continues, more muscles are employed to squeeze as much air as possible out of the body. After enlisting the internal intercostal muscles, the body then calls upon the rectus abdominis muscles (commonly known as "abs"). Located in front of and beneath the lungs, these muscles help squeeze the abdomen in an effort to expel more air from the body. If speech persists even further without air inspiration, the external oblique muscles activate. These muscles are located on the individual's sides and work to compress the torso even more. Finally, if these efforts are not enough to perform a speech act or if the note one is holding is held even longer, the latissimus dorsi is used to squeeze the very last drop of air out of the body. Located on the sides of the back, these muscles are the last resort available to anyone hoping to expel any vestige of air out of the body during speech or singing. [16]

Understanding where these muscles are and what it feels like when they are enlisted is essential for preachers who want to make the most of their speech acts. If proper breathing is essential for a preacher who wants to prevent a small or shallow voice, then understanding how to expel air from the body in the greatest capacity gives the preacher the opportunity to speak for longer without taking additional breaths. This is especially helpful in reading long passages or whenever a preacher does not want to interrupt an important series of phrases with a breath.

The ability to properly push air out of the body is also important for vocal quality. As with a brass instrument, the better one pushes air through the instrument, the better the instrument sounds. Preventing vocal problems will be discussed in more detail in the next chapter.

Exercise

In order to experience these muscles in action and actually feel when and how they are used during prolonged speech acts, consider this exercise. Stand up straight with your legs shoulder-width apart

---

[16] Ibid., 18-36. This entire discussion concerning air expiration has been adapted from Thomas J. Hixon and his collaborators.

and take a minute to breath in and out by means of the diaphragm (as instructed above). When ready, take in as much air as possible for a count of three (being sure to focus on expanding your abdomen as much as your chest) and then begin to count out loud with a strong and deep voice (you may also choose to quote a long passage or the verse of a popular rhyme). When you continue to count, be careful not to breathe in through your mouth or nose in between numbers. Eventually, you will begin to feel the involuntary squeezing of your chest, by means of the external and internal costal muscles. As counting continues (still with the same vocal quality with which you started), you will feel your abdomen tighten followed by your sides (by means of the rectus abdominis and external oblique). Finally, when you think you cannot count any higher, at about the time you must take in more air, you will feel your back compress as the latissimus dorsi contracts.

> *"Squeeze gentlemen. Don't cheat! Squeeze!"*
>
> -Doc

This exercise teaches the preacher to use these muscles during sermonic presentation instead of taking as many breaths as possible. The preachers who use this muscle system well will be able to achieve longer periods of speech in between breaths and the ability to speak for longer amounts of time with a higher quality voice without becoming winded.

The voice is one remarkable example of how fearfully and wonderfully people have been made in the image of God. Everyone with the ability to speak needs to thank God for bestowing upon them a gift that no other creature has—communication through words. No matter how pretty a bird chirps or how loudly a dog barks, no means of communication is near as sweet as the verbal communication achieved by human beings, for it is one way in which we resemble the Creator.

Preachers who understand their own unique instrument will learn to cultivate what God has given them to its fullest potential for His glory in the task of preaching. However, understanding this incredible instrument and playing it in tune are two very different things.

CHAPTER 7

Tuning the Instrument

*". . . the tongue is a small part of the body,
and yet it boasts of great things."*

-James 3:5

We are blessed at our church to have a music minister who chooses songs that introduce the congregation to the sermon that is preached every Sunday. Along with the talented ensemble of singers and gifted musicians, our music each week acts as a fitting precursor to the presentation of God's Word. However, recently something began to stick out in a negative way. The piano was out of tune. Although our pianist is top notch and all of the notes were correct, the music was suffering because the piano was not reaching its optimum pitch.

Many preachers suffer from a similar phenomenon. Though a sermon might be saturated with the Word of God, well organized, creative, and full of energy, the speaker may be speaking out of tune and using a voice that does not reflect his optimum pitch. The previous chapter explained the miracle of voicing; this chapter will address how a preacher can discover his voice, use his voice, protect his voice, and improve his voice in order that it might be used in the best possible way for the glory of God and the benefit of the congregation.

Discovering Your Voice

As stated earlier, everyone in the world has a unique voice that has been given to them by God as a tool to worship Him and spread His gospel. However, many preachers are tempted to slip into "ministerial tune," i.e., a special voice with expected preaching qualities. Too often, preachers use a voice that is severely different from their own. More often than not, they strain their voice in order to mimic a popular mentor and inflect their speech in ways they believe are more appealing to their audience. This is not necessary and can actually prove harmful to the vocal folds. For this reason, every preacher needs to discover their own voice and use it appropriately.

This is where optimum pitch comes into play. Everyone that can speak has an optimum frequency for their voice. The average male voice is around 120hz or middle C on a piano. Though many voices might be higher or lower than 120hz, this is a ballpark figure that identifies where most men normally speak.

However, because of adrenaline and the increased volume required for preaching, the tendency for most preachers is to slip into a higher voice or, for an average man, around two whole steps above middle C (E). This should be avoided at all costs.

Preachers must discover their own optimum pitch and preach in that pitch on a consistent basis so that they can avoid vocal problems. In order to discover your optimum pitch and feel as well as hear exactly what kind of voice you should use when preaching consider the following exercise.

Exercise

Gently massage your thyroid cartilage on either side by using your thumb and forefinger. While doing this, whisper a familiar verse, song, or rhyme, making sure to completely relax your throat and mouth. After whispering and massaging for around 30 seconds, break into full speech, making sure to maintain the same relaxed feeling in your throat. This is one way to identify your optimum pitch. You will discover, more often than not, that this tone is slightly lower than what you might have expected or normally use.

Using Your Voice

Maintaining one's optimum pitch during a sermonic presentation is easier said than done. All kinds of pressures, both from within and from without make it difficult to speak in one's proper vocal range. For instance, nerves as well as increased adrenaline normally will constrict the throat and contribute to a higher vocal pitch (well beyond one's optimum pitch). Also, preachers in large sanctuaries tend to over-compensate with their volume, lending to a strained voice that exceeds their natural comfort zone. In order to keep these tendencies from manifesting themselves, it is important to remember a few voicing principles.

First, proper speaking begins with proper breathing. A preacher will not preach in the right voice if he has not taken in enough air. Like fuel to a car or charge to a battery, adequate air is the source of optimum voicing. Remember, the preacher must employ the use of the diaphragm to inspire the maximum amount of air possible and then enlist the appropriate muscle groups to expel the air from the body.

> *"As you are speaking, visualize yourself*
> *pushing a firm column of air out of your lungs,*
> *through the vocal folds, and out of your mouth.*
> *Preaching requires a steady stream of air."*
>
> -Doc

Another principle to keep in mind is rate of flow. Often, preachers are unaware of how fast they are speaking and as a result can preach ahead of their audience. When a preacher speaks too fast, his voice tends to become higher and tenser. Not only does this lead to an out-of-tune voice, but it is no help to those who are receiving the message. Speaking too fast results in tense voicing and a loss of comprehension.

Finally, excitement, or lack thereof, has a tremendous impact on one's optimum pitch. When a preacher is inflecting his voice for emphasis, it is important to remember that keeping one's optimum pitch is still preferred. Though volume may fluctuate and tone may change, the optimum pitch needs to remain the same if at all possible. Too often when a preacher gets louder, the pitch slips higher. On the other hand, if a preacher is too relaxed behind the pulpit or lazy in his presentation, the pitch can drop beneath his optimum level. Whether flat or sharp, both of these problems are examples of preaching out of tune. Though these warnings may seem nit-picky, vocal abuse over a long period of time can contribute to physiological problems that result in an overly raspy voice or a weak and airy voice. This is why vocal protection, especially for pastors, is so important.

Protecting Your Voice

Recently my wife and I moved into a new home. One of the things I have taken the responsibility for is the landscaping outside. Over the last several months, one of the unlovely results of my labor has been a series of calluses accumulating on my hands from using garden tools and pulling hundreds of weeds. Friction anywhere on the skin over a long period of time results in these blisters wherever the rubbing continues for too long. The same is true of the vocal folds.

The rapid movement of the vocal folds during speech is expected and necessary for audible communication. However, each one's voice is designed to achieve its optimum pitch. Therefore, whenever a voice is strained for too long, the vocal folds can form blisters and calluses along their edges. This is because the folds are rubbing against each other in an unnatural way over an extended period of time. When the vocal folds develop calluses on their edges, the uneven bumps create imperfect gaps between the two folds when they come together to achieve speech. This allows air to escape between vibrations, giving the voice a raspy quality.

The only way to fix calluses that have formed on the vocal folds is to surgically remove them. After these operations, the patients are told to refrain from speaking for months! What preacher can afford that? Procedures like this are risky and often do not solve the long term problem. Inevitably, when surgeons remove a callus, more is removed than necessary, allowing air to escape where the edge of the vocal fold used to be (and where the callus was). This is why preachers must learn to use their voice properly. Prevention through cultivation of the optimum pitch is the prescription all preachers must take in order to avoid these and other problems.

Improving Your Voice

Now that the preacher understands how to discover his optimum pitch and why it is important to cultivate this pitch during his sermons, vocal avoidances need to be addressed. The following is a list of common vocal infractions that can make a sermon out of tune. Though these may not contribute to vocal abuse, these infractions often distract congregations or hurt their comprehension of what is being said. Alleviating any or all of these potential problems will result in an improved preaching voice and better presentation of God's Word.

Dropped Phrases-Dropped phrases occur when a preacher fails to end a sentence with the same volume that began the sentence. Sometimes, especially in long phrases, preachers may run out of air and compensate for this by making the last few words softer. This causes the sentence to trail off and can leave people saying, "What did he say?" or "I didn't catch the end of that?" In order to avoid this, the preacher needs to be sure he is taking in enough air and using his squeezing muscles to make the most of his speech acts. Make sure to always push toward the end of the phrases.

> *"Don't run out of steam. The end of your sentence*
> *is just as important as the beginning"*
>
> -Doc

Inarticulation-Problems of articulation differ from person to person and can result in a loss of comprehension. Sometimes in-articulation happens because a preacher is not opening his mouth enough for the air and words to come out clearly. This makes the preacher sound muffled and creates a mumbling effect.

Another example of in-articulation is witnessed when a preacher may not be adequately forming the words with his lips, tongue, and teeth. This produces a slurred or sloppy pronunciation of words. Therefore, a preacher needs to be sure that he is allowing air to move freely through a wide open mouth and that he is over enunciating his words so that everyone in the congregation understands what is being said.

Monotony-The last thing any preacher wants is to sound like is Charlie Brown's teacher. However, many preachers speak in a monotone voice that runs the risk of putting people to sleep. This happens when there is a lack of voice inflection and variety in speech. Sermons need to be lively in their presentation as well as in their information. Preachers must be sure that they are inflecting their voice appropriately in order to present a sermon that is as easy and interesting to listen to as it is to understand.

Nasality—Nasality takes place when the air moving from the lungs is allowed to register in the sinuses to an unreasonable extent. This results in a voice that sounds like it is coming from someone with a cold or who has his or her nose plugged. A helpful way of making sure that the sinuses are not dominating the sound of the voice involves pinching the nose shut and working to achieve the same vocal quality that happens when one is speaking normally.

Vocal Fry-One other voice infraction to watch out for is vocal fry. When a preacher has a raspy quality to his voice, he is experiencing this phenomenon. Often this takes place at the end of phrases or sentences when the preacher runs out of air. Slipping into vocal fry like this eventually leads to a raspy voice and is another example of what can happen when there is a lack of breath support. In order to combat this, preachers need to focus on pushing air out at the end of their phrases in order to avoid a raspy sound. No matter how discreet, vocal fry must be avoided as much as possible.

"Take a couple of deep breaths and be ready to come out of the starting gate with good vocal quality. Are you ready? You're On!"

-Doc

Understanding the voice and how it works is one thing, but understanding one's own voice and cultivating its most perfect sound is something else entirely. Although this may seem like a lot to keep in mind, preachers who record their sermons and listen to themselves carefully will be able to identify any vocal problems they have and work on fixing them so that they might become well-tuned instruments in the hand of Almighty God.

Prevention of vocal abuse and correction of problems is the responsibility every preacher must own in order to achieve longevity in their preaching ministry and the very best voice for the greatest number of years. For many who are reading these pages, God has appointed you to preach the Word. Shouldn't you desire through His grace and your training to make the most of this sacred calling? No one would play in a concert hall with an out-of-tune instrument. So do not go before God's people with an out-of-tune sermon.

EPILOGUE

As defined in the early portion of this resource, expository preaching, that is, preaching in its truest and purest sense, is an outgrowth of a man's immersing himself within a passage in intensive study, finding the proper limits of that passage, discovering the arguments of the passage, organizing a sermonic outline drawn directly from the passage, and then endeavoring to set forth to his hearers the message of that passage in such a manner as to effect change in the lives of those listening. One way to accomplish this sacred task has been the subject of expertise and study that one of God's heroes has been proliferating for the last fifty years. His teaching has now been made available to you.

The three overarching units that Dr. Fink has taught and have been summarized in this resource work together in order to accomplish the task of preaching in an efficient and sure-fire way. Understanding the primacy of God's Word reflected in discreet organization, refining the sermon with presentational polish, and cultivating one's own voice will leave preachers on solid footing whenever they approach their pulpits on Sunday morning. As Dr. Fink would remind his classes in every one of his syllabuses,

> *"If you honestly do the very best that you can,*
> *you probably will do well in this course."*
>
> -Doc

Applied to the subject of this study, if preachers honestly apply the principles in these pages the very best that they can, more often than not they will exposit God's Word accurately, creatively, and clearly to any audience God brings their way.

It is my prayer that many preachers would learn from and apply these encouragements in much the same way I learned them and continue to apply them in my ministry. Do not settle for your opinion, aim for the message His Word teaches. Do not upstage the Speaker, give focus to what God is saying. Do not take on another's voice, allow God to use your voice for His glory.

Though this resource does not pretend to exhaust the subject of preaching in any or all of its many nuances, it is my hope that those who read this may think of it as a foundation upon which to build their own style.

> *"We are not in the business of producing preachers*
> *who resemble each other in a cookie-cutter approach;*
> *but developing individual messengers of God's Word*
> *that understand these significant guidelines and*
> *apply them appropriately for the Glory of God."*
>
> -Doc

Take what you want, add what you like, but respect all that is here in order that God's Word may continue to speak in profound ways through those He's appointed to carry the message of the Gospel to the ends of the earth.

APPENDIX #1

Concise Grammar Compendium

Action Verb: Words that explain or describe what a subject is doing.

John 11:35—"Jesus **wept**."

Adjective: Words that describe a noun or another adjective.

Psalm 84:2b—". . . My heart and my flesh sing for joy to the **living** God."

Adverb: Words used primarily to express how something is done and thereby modifying the verb. These most often end in "ly."

Psalm 147:15—"He sends forth His command to the earth; His word runs very **swiftly**"

Article: Words that introduce or distinguish nouns ("a," "an," and "the").

Matthew 6:16—"whenever you fast, do not put on **a** gloomy face as **the** hypocrites do . . ."

Conjunction: Words used to connect nouns, phrases, or clauses ("and," "but," "because," "for," "that," etc.).

Romans 1:18-19—"For the wrath of God is revealed from heaven against all ungodliness **and** unrighteousness of men who suppress the truth in unrighteousness, **because** that which is known about God is evident within them; **for** God made it evident to them."

Declarative Sentence: A sentence that communicates a fact or state of being.

> *John 8:12*—". . . **I am the light of the world; He who follows Me will not walk in the darkness, but will have the Light of life.**"

Demonstrative Pronoun: Pronouns that seem to point to referred nouns ("this," "that," "these," "those").

> *James 1:27*—"Pure and undefiled religion in the sight of our God and Father is **this:** to visit orphans and widows in their distress, and to keep oneself unstained by the world."

Dependent Clause: Phrases that contain a subject and verb which describe an independent clause. These cannot stand by themselves and include relative clauses, participial clauses, and infinitive clauses.

> *Ruth 1:18*—"**When she saw that she was determined to go with her,** she said no more to her."

Direct Object: Words that communicate who or what is immediately affected by the verb.

> *Exodus 3:5*—"Then He said, 'Do not come near here; remove your **sandals** from your feet; for the place on which you are standing is holy ground."

Exclamatory Sentence: A sentence that proclaims something in a heightened emotional tone.

> *Galatians 2:17*—". . . **May it never be!**"

Future Tense: A verb tense used to communicate what has yet to take place.

> *1 Thessalonians 4:16*—"For the Lord Himself **will descend** from heaven with a shout, with the voice of *the* archangel and with the trumpet of God, and the dead in Christ **will rise** first."

Imperative Sentence: A sentence that acts as a command or request.

> *Exodus 20:12*—"**Honor your father and your mother**, . . ."

Imperfect Tense: The verb tense that expresses action in the past that has not been completed, action that occurs habitually, or action that takes place over an indefinite period of time.

> *Mark 9:1*—"And Jesus **was saying** to them . . ."

Independent Clause: Phrases that contain a subject and verb and can exist as a complete sentence.

> *2 Corinthians 4:7*—"**But we have this treasure in earthen vessels,** so that the surpassing greatness of the power will be of God and not from ourselves."

Indirect Object: The person or thing that an action is done to or the recipient of the action.

1 Timothy 3:14—"I am writing these things to **you,** hoping to come to **you** before long."

Infinitive: A verb form that functions as a noun or is used with other verbs in order to name an action or state without specifying the subject ("to . . .").

1 Timothy 2:8—"Therefore I want the men in every place **to pray,** lifting up holy hands, without wrath and dissension."

Interrogative Sentence: An expression of inquiry that asks for a response (a.k.a. a question).

1 Peter 3:13—"**Who is there to harm you if you prove zealous for what is good?**"

Intransitive Verb: Verb forms that do not take direct objects.

Genesis 41:1—"Now it **happened** at the end of two full years that Pharaoh had a dream, and behold, he **was standing** by the Nile."

Modifier: Anything that describes, explains, or clarifies a word or a phrase (adjectives, adverbs, articles, prepositional phrases, participial clauses, relative clauses, etc.).

Song of Solomon 2:13—"**The fig** tree has ripened **its** figs, and **the** vines **in blossom** have given forth **their** fragrance. Arise **my** darling, **my beautiful** one, and come along!"

Noun: A word that communicates a person, place, thing or idea.

Luke 1:80—"And the **child** continued to grow and to become strong in **spirit**, and he lived in the **deserts** until the **day** of his public **appearance** to **Israel**."

Object of Preposition: The word that comes after a preposition and completes the prepositional phrase.

Isaiah 53:5—"But He was pierced through for our **transgressions**, He was crushed for our **iniquities**; the chastening for our **well-being** *fell* upon **Him**."

Participle: A verbal form that behaves as an adjective or noun.

Daniel 3:19—". . . He answered by **giving** orders to heat the furnace seven times more than it was usually heated."

Participial Clause: A dependent clause whose verbal form is a participle.

Acts 3:11—"**While he was clinging to Peter and John**, all the people ran together to them at the so-called portico of Solomon, full of amazement."

Past Tense: A verb tense that communicates what took place in the past.

Romans 1:24—"Therefore, God **gave them over** in the lusts of their hearts to impurity, so that their bodies would be dishonored among them."

Perfect Tense: A verb tense that communicates completed action.

Ephesians 2:13—"But now in Christ Jesus you who formerly were far off **have been brought near** by the blood of Christ."

Possessive Pronoun: A word that is substituted for noun that suggests ownership of the word it modifies ("my," "your," "their," etc.).

Psalm 85:1-2—"O Lord, You showed favor to **Your** land; You restored the captivity of Jacob. You forgave the iniquity of **Your** people; You covered all **their** sin."

Predicate Adjective: An adjective that describes the subject following a stative verb.

Matthew 4:2—"And after He had fasted forty days and forty nights, He then became **hungry**."

Predicate Nominative: A noun that renames the subject following a stative verb.

Psalm 23:1—"The Lord is my **shepherd,** I shall not want."

Preposition: The word that introduces a prepositional phrase. These include words that introduce direction ("to," "into"), location ("in," "up," "under"), time ("yesterday," "last week"), association ("with"), agency ("through," "by"), or clarification ("of").

Deuteronomy 34:1—"Now Moses went up **from** the plains of Moab **to** Mount Nebo, **to** the top **of** Pisgah, which is opposite Jericho. And the Lord showed him all the land, Gilead **as far as** Dan."

Prepositional Phrase: Phrases that communicate direction, location, time, association, agency, or clarification of a verb or noun.

> *Genesis 1:1*—"**In the beginning** God created the heavens and the earth."

Present Tense: The tense that communicates action taking place now or action that is in progress.

> *Luke 9:48*—"and said to them, 'Whoever **receives** this child in my name **receives** Me, and whoever **receives** Me **receives** Him who sent Me; for the one who **is** least among all of you, this **is** the one who **is** great.'"

Pronoun: A word used to replace a noun in a given context ("he," "you," "me," "anybody," "it," "ours," etc.).

> *John 4:32*—"But **He** said to **them**, '**I** have food to eat that **you** do not know about.'"

Proper Noun: Names of specific places, people, written works, etc. that are capitalized.

> *Revelation 1:11*—". . . 'Write in a book what you see, and send it to the seven churches: to **Ephesus** and to **Smyrna** and to **Pergamum** and to **Thyatira** and to **Sardis** and to **Philadelphia** and to **Laodicea**.'"

Relative Pronoun: A pronoun that introduces a relative clause ("that," "who," "which," etc.).

> *1 Corinthians 11:23*—"For I received from the Lord that **which** I also delivered to you, that the Lord Jesus in the night in **which** He was betrayed took bread;"

Relative Clause: A clause that describes a noun or pronoun in the context by means of a relative pronoun and verbal form.

> *Philippians 3:20-21*—"For our citizenship is in heaven, from which also we eagerly wait for a Savior, the Lord Jesus Christ; **who will transform the body of our humble state into conformity with the body of His glory, . . .**"

Stative Verb: Verbs of being ("is," "are," "be," "becomes," etc.).

> *Jeremiah 32:38*—"They **shall be** My people, and I **will be** their God;"

Subject: The noun that is performing the action of a clause.

> *Mark 9:9*—"As they were coming down from the mountain, **He** gave them orders not to relate to anyone what they had seen, until the Son of Man rose from the dead."

Transitive Verbs: Verb forms that take direct objects.

> *Hebrews 11:17*—"By faith Abraham, when he was tested, **offered up** Isaac, and he who had received the promises **was offering up** his only begotten son."

APPENDIX #2

Diagramming 101

The following is a diagram of basic sentence parts.

| Subject | Main Verb | Direct object |

In the above diagram, it is important to remember that not all verbs will take direct objects. Some might describe what is pictured above a "baseline" because it illustrates the fundamental parts of most sentences. Diagrams of verbs that are intransitive will simply ignore the direct object portion of the diagram and the line that separates the main verb from where the direct object would go. An example of this would be John 11:35.

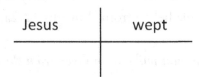

The following is a diagram of a sentence with a stative verb ("is," "are," "becomes," etc.)

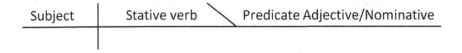

Notice that in this diagram, there is a slanted line that separates the predicate adjective/nominative from the stative verb. This demonstrates that the predicate is describing or renaming the subject as the line points in that direction.

The following is a diagram of a sentence that demonstrates where common modifiers would go.

Subject	Main Verb		Direct Object
Article	Adverb		Adjective
	Preposition	Object of Preposition	Pronoun

This diagram shows that all modifying elements of the subject are placed on shelves pointing to the left while all other modifiers pertaining to the verb and object point to the right. This helps separate the subject from the rest of the sentence.

Also, adverbs and prepositional phrases (composed of a preposition and its object) typically modify verbs (with the exception of the preposition "of"). This example demonstrates that the way to diagram a preposition and its object resembles how one diagrams a verb and its object.

No matter how many modifiers modify a particular word, it is important that each be given its own shelf immediately beneath that which they modify in the order that they appear in the verse. Consider the example below from Proverbs 12:2a.

"A good man will obtain favor from the Lord"

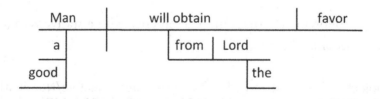

Both "a" and "good" modify the subject "man" who "will obtain" in the future the "favor" that the verse is talking about. Also, "from the Lord" is a prepositional phrase that describes from whom the man will obtain this favor and therefore modifies the action taking place in the sentence. This is why the prepositional phrase is placed beneath the verb.

However, what if there are multiple subjects, verbs, direct objects, etc.? In cases where there are multiple items being discussed, a "fork" must be placed in the diagram wherever necessary as suggested by this example from John 14:6b.

". . . I am the way, and the truth, and the life . . ."

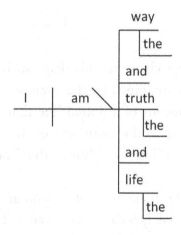

The stative verb "am" requires a slanted line in between it and the predicate nominatives being used here. Jesus is renamed by each of these three things along with their articles as expressed in this diagram along with the conjunction "and."

Conjunctions like "and," "but," or "because" can also be used to join two independent clauses, each with their own verb, subject, and object. The diagram for Acts 5:18 illustrates how this is diagrammed.

"They laid hands on the apostles and
put them in a public jail"

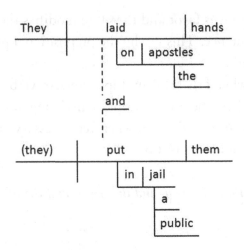

Each independent clause in this diagram is shown as its own unit. However, they are joined by the conjunction "and" as shown in the diagram by means of a dotted line that connects the main verb of the first clause to the main verb of the second clause. This can also be done when "because," "but," "that," or "for" connect two independent clauses.

Another important element of grammar that needs to be diagrammed appropriately is the relative clause. These are dependent clauses that begin with "who," "whom," or "which." Because they are not the main action taking place, they are attached to the base line of the independent clause that they modify. However, because they contain a verb, each relative clause must contain its own lesser baseline that is added to the diagram on stilts beneath the word or phrase it modifies. The diagram for Galatians 6:6 reveals how relative clauses are diagrammed.

> *"The one who is taught the word is to share all*
> *good things with the one who teaches him."*

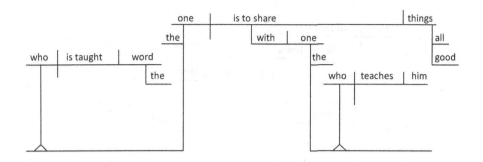

This diagram reveals one independent idea, "one is to share all good things." Everything else about the verse modifies this clause. "Who is taught the word" reveals who the "one" is and therefore is placed beneath the subject. Because this phrase contains a verb, it must be placed on its own baseline on stilts as shown (along with its direct object). The same is true with "who teaches him" and its relation to "the one" in the prepositional phrase of the verse. A good rule of thumb to remember is that "who" is always the subject while "whom" is always the direct object of a dependent clause. "Which" can serve in either capacity. Infinitive phrases like "to run" or "to speak" are also diagrammed on stilts wherever they are being used (either as a modifier, direct object, or subject). Participial phrases work the same way.

Discourse or larger quotes can often be difficult to diagram. Very literally, what someone says is the direct object of the verb "said" or "proclaims." Therefore, instead of diagramming an entire discourse on the direct object portion of the diagram by means of an enormous structure of stilts and dotted lines, arrows can be used in order to symbolize that a discourse or an extended quote is present within the text. Arrows like this can be used when the word "that" introduces discourse also. Remember this arrow whenever phrases like "He said," "He prayed," or "they thought" are used. Here is a simple example of this from Luke 17:14a.

"When He saw them, He said to them, 'Go and show yourselves to the priest.'"

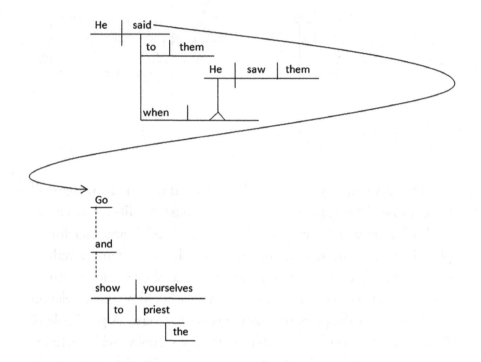

This diagram reveals several important things. First, a dependent clause is used to describe the time that Jesus said what He did in this verse, "when He saw them." This dependent clause is a prepositional phrase led by "when" and its object, "he saw this." Because the object contains a verb, it must be displayed on stilts as shown above.

Second, this verse contains discourse. The quote, "go and show yourselves to the priest" is literally the object of the verb "said" (it tells the reader what Jesus communicated). However, instead of putting the content of Jesus' speech where the direct object traditionally goes, the arrow points to the content of Jesus' speech as the direct object.

Third, both "go" and "show" are independent clauses as they are imperatives (commands) with an understood subject ("you"). Because of this, they are connected by the conjunction "and" in the way described earlier for joining independent thoughts.

One final introduction that needs to be made in this diagramming guide includes vocative words or introductory words used to draw attention. These include, but are not limited to "behold," "brethren," "friends," etc. When words like this are used to introduce a passage or verse, they are diagrammed separate from the main clause as shown in this example from John 1:29.

"The next day he saw Jesus coming to him and said, 'Behold, the Lamb of God who takes away the sins of the world!'"

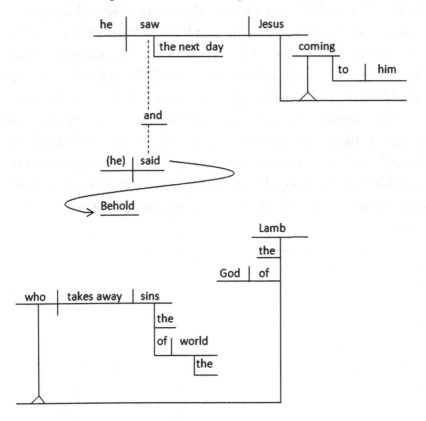

This verse illustrates the majority of what has been taught in this diagrammatical tutorial. The independent clause "he saw Jesus" is modified by the prepositional phrase "the next day" telling us when John saw Jesus. The modifying verbal noun "coming" describes something about Jesus. This independent clause is connected to the next independent idea "(he) said" by the conjunction "and" and the dotted lines connecting verb to verb. "Said" implies a quote or discourse which is demonstrated by the arrow that points to "behold" and the remainder of the verse.

In the quote portion of the verse, there is no main verb for the subject "Lamb." This is demonstrated in the diagram accordingly. Also, the phrase "who takes away the sins of the world" describes more about this Lamb along with article "the" and the prepositional phrase "of God." "Behold" is not a part of the main clause and therefore is shown to introduce the thought by placing it before the rest of the diagram on its own line. Other words that are diagrammed before the rest of the verse in this manner include "therefore," "for," and "but" (when "but" is not being used to join independent clauses).

This tutorial does not begin to illustrate all of the different diagrammatical nuances that a student will come across in the Bible. Instead, this serves as a starting point for those who hope to master this skill in Bible study. For those who desire to delve deeper into diagramming, please consult Lee Kantenwein's *Diagrammatical Analysis.*

APPENDIX #3

Plural Noun Possibilities

Abilities
Accounts
Acknowledgments
Actions
Activities
Addresses
Affirmations
Arguments
Aspects
Attempts
Axioms
Callings
Challenges
Characters
Characteristics
Charges
Choruses
Commands
Comparisons
Conclusions
Conditions
Conflicts
Contrasts
Cues
Demands

Demonstrations
Difficulties
Directions
Doctrines
Elements
Encouragements
Examples
Exclamations
Features
Fundamentals
Gifts
Greetings
Idols
Illusions
Illustrations
Imperatives
Inquiries
Institutions
Instructions
Introductions
Lamentations
Lessons
Lies
Manifestations
Methods

Miracles
Models
Movements
Numbers
Observations
Paradoxes
Parts
Paths
Perspectives
Phases
Positions
Powers
Presentations
Principles
Problems
Prohibitions
Promises
Qualifications
Questions
Reasons
Refrains
Reservations

Results
Revelations
Salutations
Sayings
Scenes
Solutions
Spectacles
Stages
Stanzas
Statements
Steps
Suggestions
Symptoms
Teachings
Temptations
Testimonies
Troubles
Truths
Voices
Verses
Ways
Witnesses

APPENDIX #4

Passage Sermon Example

Introduction: Michael W. Smith has a song entitled *This is your Time* that was inspired by initial reports concerning a girl named Cassie Bernall who was killed in the Columbine shootings. According to some who were there, she was asked by one of the gunman "do you believe in God?" She answered, "yes" and was immediately murdered. The voices involved in this story echo the voices heard 7 feet above Golgotha 2000 years ago. Faced with certain death, what would you say if asked the same question Cassie answered? Interestingly enough, all of the answers to this question can be divided into two distinct categories that are represented by the two thieves who hung on either side of Christ. Their voices heard in the midst of their suffering are emblematic of the choices people make concerning God in the midst of their suffering today. Listen carefully to what you hear in between the gasps for air and the vociferous cries of the spectators in Luke 23:39-43.

Proposition: Today we are going to listen carefully to THREE VOICES heard 7 feet above Golgotha from Luke 23:39-43.

    I.   VOICE #1: THE VOICE OF RAGE-23:39
   II. VOICE #2: THE VOICE OF REASON-23:40-42
  III. VOICE #3: THE VOICE OF REDEMPTION-23:43

I. VOICE #1: THE VOICE OF RAGE-23:39

A. The Speaker is Identified-23:39—". . . One of the criminals who were hanged there . . ."

> **"who were hanged"**-(Aorist, Passive, Participle, Masculine, Genitive, Plural, κρεμαννυμι-Adjectival) Lit. "to crucify." "Hanging" was a euphemism for the practice of crucifying on a cross. In fact, the word for cross was anathema in many social circles and in polite conversation. So horrible were the characteristics of crucifixion that it was not something people referred to directly.

> Note: Crucifixion was viewed by ancient writers as the cruelest and most barbaric of punishments. Recent historical and archaeological studies have helped bring a realistic sense of crucifixion's horrors. The bone fragments of a crucified individual were discovered in 1968 and revealed that the victim's feet were each nailed laterally to the beam. In many cases, both the feet and wrists were nailed to the crossbeam the victim carried. This would have taken place after the victim was stripped of his clothes to increase the humiliation. After victims were nailed to the crossbeam, the structure was raised high enough for the criminal's feet to clear the ground and then placed on a stake. Most guess that Jesus' cross stood about 7 feet high. This method of execution was designed for one thing, a slow and painful death. Death by crucifixion was a result of loss of blood, exposure, exhaustion, and suffocation, as the victim tried to lift himself

to breathe. Sometimes, victims would linger for days in agony! In fact, the meaning of the word "excruciating" is derived from the Latin *excruciatus*, meaning "out of the cross."

Note: Though many tend to focus their attention on Jesus in the center of the Golgotha scene, it is important to remember that Jesus was one of three currently facing this unthinkable horror. Given the nature of their current predicament, it is no wonder that one of the thieves speaks up and in his rage says what he can in the midst of his shallow breaths.

B. The Speech is Characterized-23:39b—". . . was hurling abuse at Him . . ."

"hurling abuse"-(Imperfect, Active, Indicative, 3rd Person, Singular, Βλασφημεω-Progressive) The word used here for "hurling abuse" is the same word for "blaspheme" which means "to speak against someone in such a way as to harm or injure his or her reputation." The nature of the imperfect verb seems to suggest that the thief was spending his last moments blaspheming Jesus constantly.

Note: Though this comment was damning in retrospect, one might expect a voice like this in the midst of such agony. The first thief's voice illustrates one of the choices everyone has in a situation like this—rage.

Reflection: In many ways this first thief represents a large sector of humanity. Those who in the face of suffering shake an angry fist at the God they do not even believe in find a sympathizer in this man and might even be caught saying what he says here, "Are you not the Christ? Save Yourself and us!"

C. The Speech is Revealed-23:39c—". . . , saying, 'Are you not the Christ? Save Yourself and us!' . . ."

"**Save**"-(Aorist, Active, Imperative, 2nd Person, Singular, σωζω-Request/Command) Although many uses of the word "save" allude to God's work of salvation, given the context and the blasphemous nature of his remark, there is no way that this thief is making a legitimate plea for salvation. Instead, he is requesting rescue from his current predicament. In his limited view of Jesus, he sarcastically calls upon Him (in light of who he claims to be) to miraculously provide a means of escaping the death they all face.

Reflection: This hellacious cry echoes throughout the generations among those who fail to believe in Jesus Christ. Seeing no way of escape from their death or agony, instead of reaching out to Jesus in faith for salvation, they question Him, His love, and His sovereignty, and in their unbelief grasp only at straws. Calvin says of this raging blasphemer, "This objection is directed against God Himself; just as wicked men, when they do not obtain what they wish, would willingly tear God from heaven. They ought indeed, to be tamed to humility by strokes;

but this shows that the wicked heart, which no punishments can bend, is hard like iron." The voice of rage says, "There is no God, look how much I'm hurting! If there was a God, why would he allow me this pain?"

Transition: However, there was a second voice heard 7ft. above Golgotha.

II. VOICE #2: THE VOICE OF REASON-23:40-42

A. The Speaker is Identified-23:40a—". . . But the other answered, and rebuking him said . . ."

"**rebuking**"-(Present, Active, Participle, Nominative, Masculine, Singular, επιτιμαω-Adv, Manner) The second thief expresses strong disapproval of what the first thief is saying.

Note: The second thief cannot put up with the insistent blaspheming of Jesus. Instead of holding his tongue or saving his breaths for himself as he reels in pain, he openly rebukes the statements being made on the other side of the skull rock.

Reflection: In what this second criminal says, the reader is made aware of another way, the proper way, to view one's own predicament before Christ. Though in the first man's response to pain and agony we heard the voice of a raging blasphemer, here we observe the surprising and yet unmistakable voice of reason.

B. The Speech is Given-23:40b-42

1. **Rebuke of the Blasphemer-23:40b**—". . . . 'Do you not even fear God, since you are under the same sentence of condemnation? . . .'"

   > **"fear"**-(Present, Middle, Indicative, 2nd Person, Singular, φοβεω-<u>Progressive</u>) "be afraid," "respect," "worship."

   > <u>Note:</u> The first statement uttered by this second voice is a statement of rebuke. "Do you not even fear God, since you are under the same sentence of condemnation?" In other words, the second thief asks the first, "Does not your present condemnation compel you to fear God?" In this statement, the second robber is hoping that the first recognizes that death is coming soon, and it is no time to be blaspheming an innocent man. Though their present predicament was desperate and difficult, it would not compare to what he would feel before God at the judgment seat. Though he was now feeling the results of being condemned by the Roman government, he would soon discover what it would feel like to be condemned by God Himself!

   > <u>Reflection:</u> Though this rebuke was designed to put the fear of God into the first thief, there is no evidence that suggests it was successful. Instead, his hard heart hardened. He is no different than many in our world today. Instead of fearing God many abstain from Him, harden themselves, and fall into condemnation. Any reasonable person

would understand that they should fear most the God who can kill body and spirit.

> Matt. 10:28—*"Do not fear those who kill the body but are unable to kill the soul; but rather fear Him who is able to destroy both soul and body in hell."*

2. **Reminder of guilt-23:41**—". . . And we indeed *are suffering* justly, for we are receiving what we deserve for our deeds; but this man has done nothing wrong.' . . ."

> **"are receiving"**-(Present, Active, Indicative, 1st Person, Plural, απολαμβανω-Progressive) "For we are receiving what we deserve." The idea of receiving here is "experiencing some event or state, often with the implication of something negatively valued."

> Note: The second thief understands that what they are experiencing is exactly what they "deserve." He acknowledges here that the punishment which was common to all three was "justly" inflicted on him and his companion, but not on Christ. Instead, He had been dragged to the punishment of death, not by His crime, but by the cruelty of His enemies. The second thief reasonably concludes, in light of his crime, that the punishment he is suffering at present is natural and expected, not something surprising or unjust. Unlike his companion thief, who thought God to be unjust and/or unreal, this man recognizes that the real injustice is being exercised on the man in the middle.

Reflection: As mentioned earlier, this man might represent all who reasonably conclude that their present sufferings, agonies, and even anticipated death are a result of their own sinful choices, depravity, and the extensive wickedness that infects the entire fallen world. The difficulty they face and the hardships around them are understood by these as the product of sin in their lives, the lives of others, and creation itself. Therefore, what they are experiencing and will experience after death without Christ is not understood as unjust, but the proper penalty assigned to each of them. The only thing they can do in light of this is call upon the Lord.

3. **Request for Salvation-23:42**—". . . and he was saying, 'Jesus, remember me when You come in Your kingdom!' . . ."

Note: Calling upon the Lord is exactly what is demonstrated by the second thief in this passage, "Jesus, remember me when You come in Your kingdom!"

"remember"-(Aorist, Passive, Imperative, 2nd Person, Singular, μιμνησκομαι-Request) When this thief requests Jesus' remembrance, he is not simply asking Jesus to recall information; he is asking Jesus to recall and as a result to respond in an appropriate manner (the idea being to bring him with Him to the kingdom).

Note: In this phrase, readers everywhere are given one of the most remarkable and striking examples of faith ever recorded! This thief had not been educated in the ways of Christ, but instead had given himself up to a life of sin and endeavored to rid himself of any sense of right and wrong. However, here he suddenly rises higher than all the apostles and other disciples whom the Lord Himself had taken time to instruct and adores Christ as King and calls to be invited to His kingdom! He does this while bleeding out and gasping for air on a cross! All credit for such a display of faith must go to the Holy Spirit, who, upon the thief's understanding of his sin and necessary implications thereof, supplied what was necessary to make this quantum leap to saving faith.

Reflection: Those who understand their sin and its effects are able to understand Jesus' saving power for them by means of the Holy Spirit. In this we learn that those who place their faith in Jesus Christ are reaching a reasonable conclusion—Jesus is the only means of escaping the sting of death and having eternal life. The voice of reason says, "I am responsible for my actions, expect the consequences, and desperately need Jesus to save me."

Transition: We have heard two contrasting voices so far. Thank goodness that there was a third voice heard that day.

III. VOICE #3: THE VOICE OF REDEMPTION-23:43

A. The Speaker is Identified-23:43a—". . . And He said to him, . . ."

Note: Do not forget that Jesus is suffering under the same excruciating pain these two thieves are experiencing. He is the source of the third voice in the unique conversation taking place 7 feet or so above the crowd of spectators. In His response to what has been said, it is significant to notice that Jesus addresses only the second thief and ignores the first. These same responses can be expected by those who call out to Him in faith and who curse His name today! What Jesus expresses to the thief of faith is none other than the voice of redemption.

B. The Speech is Given-23:43b—". . . 'Truly I say to you, today you shall be with Me in Paradise' . . ."

Note: To the reasonable thief Jesus says, "truly I say to you, today you shall be with Me in Paradise." This promise reveals that Jesus, though presently humiliated before the onlookers, was still the powerful Savior of the world who was capable of bringing life out of death and fulfilling every facet of His office. This thief could expect life after death that very day with Jesus in Paradise.

Note: "Paradise" is a word meaning heaven. Death is not defeat for those who belong to Jesus Christ; it is the beginning of life with God in a more profound way. This is what the second thief could expect following his last breath. In fact, anyone who turns to Jesus, even in the last moments of his or her life, is granted fellowship with Him for eternity thereafter.

Romans 10:13—*"Whoever calls upon the name of the Lord shall be saved."*

Reflection: Jesus has always been about awarding faith with grace. Here, he awards the faith of a thief at his execution with the grace of eternal life with Him in heaven. This same grace is available today to all who call upon Him, expecting to hear the voice of redemption. The voice of redemption says, "This world and its sufferings are not all that there is. Call upon me and know eternal life."

Conclusion: Three voices clearly heard 7 feet above Golgotha one fateful day 2000 years ago—a voice of rage that blasphemed all the way to hell, a voice of reason that placed faith in a dying Messiah, and a voice of redemption promising salvation from death. This scene of horror and pain calls to mind the horror and pain experienced by all in this world. Like these three, we are on our way to death, living in the midst of evil and injustice, feeling the very real effects of sin along the way. In light of this, there are two choices. To those who speak of God in rage, who do not believe in God or can't for the life of them understand why anyone would trust in a good God while there is so much suffering I say this: consider that God Himself understands the effects of sin, injustice, and death. He died in the worst possible way and did not deserve any bit of it! We suffer because we are sinful. He suffered though He sinned not! To those who speak of God with reason, who understand their responsibility and the very real results of their depravity I say this: call upon the name of the Lord in faith and He will save you from the death and punishment we all deserve. This is your time. What will God hear your voice say?

APPENDIX #5

Topical Sermon Example

Introduction: "Armageddon," "Pandemonium," "Apocalypse," "Tribulation," and "Second Coming" are buzz words many in both the secular realm and the church world like to use to spark debate, sell books, and raise questions. However, words like this are met with different reactions from different types of people. The same terms that instill hope in Jesus' return for believers lead to confusion for those who don't believe in the Bible. However, how much do we really know about Christ's Second Coming? Do we really understand what it is about, or do we flippantly discuss it based on a movie we've seen or novel we've read? The writer of Hebrews describes how Christ and what He has to offer is better in all of its parts. This includes the hope and benefit believers will one day find in Christ's Second Coming. The author of Hebrews discusses this future event and the hope that it gives in chapter 9 verse 28.

Proposition: Let us ask FIVE QUESTIONS concerning the topic of the Second Coming of Christ that can be answered in Hebrews 9:28.

    I. QUESTION #1: WHO IS RETURNING?—9:28a
    II. QUESTIONS #2: ON WHAT GROUNDS IS HE RETURNING?-9:28b-c
    III. QUESTION #3: WHY IS HE RETURNING?-9:28f-g
    IV. QUESTION #4: WHEN IS HE RETURNING?-9:28d-e
    V. QUESTION #5: WHO IS HE RETURNING FOR?—9:28h-i

I. QUESTION #1: WHO IS RETURNING?-9:28a—"so Christ . . ."

> Acts 1:11—". . . 'Men of Galilee, why do you stand looking into the sky? This Jesus, who has been taken up from you into heaven, will come in just the same way as you have watched him go into heaven."

> Note: Christ is the one returning, there isn't a question about it. It is He who ascended and He who will one day return. The word, "Christ" references Jesus' redemptive work as the anointed one and Messiah who was anticipated in the Old Testament and realized in the Gospels. The same Christ the patriarchs prophesied and the disciples experienced will come again.

> Transition: However, on what grounds is He returning?

II. QUESTION #2: ON WHAT GROUNDS IS HE RETURNING?-9:28b-c

A. The Action-9:28b—". . . Having been offered . . ."

> **"having been offered"**-(Aorist, Passive, Participle, Nominative, Masculine, Singular, προσφερω-Adv. Causal) There are several things to consider about this participle. First, it describes a definite action (as suggested by the aorist tense). The grounds for His return are based in His completed action of redemption on the earth. Second, the passive voice of this verb suggests received action. In other words, Christ was offered by God as a sacrifice for sins. The

action of His offering was happening to Him, not as though He was forced, but that He was willfully conforming to the will of His father. Third, the participle is singular. Christ was offered only once. That is all it took. His offering on the cross was final in all of its parts and acts as the basis for His return.

Hebrews 7:27—*"who needs not die daily, like those high priests, to offer up sacrifices, first for His own sins and then for the sins of the people, because this He did once for all when He offered up Himself."*

B. The Purpose-9:28c—". . . to bear the sins of many . . ."

Note: Christ came to the world, in part, "to bear the sins of many." Those who trust in Him can enjoy salvation of their soul because He bore the sins of the world. The second advent of Christ necessarily depends on His first advent which existed to accomplish this redemption.

Transition: If the problem of sin has been dealt with in Jesus' first advent, why would He be returning again?

III. QUESTION #3: WHY IS HE RETURNING?-9:28f-g

A. The Purpose-9:28f—". . . for salvation . . ."

Note: The Second Advent of Christ will involve bringing completed salvation. Christ will redeem the body—the flesh which is currently subject to the bondage of corruption. While Jesus' first coming resulted in the justification of sin (the realized component of salvation), His Second Coming will result in the glorification of the believer (the future component of salvation).

Philippians 1:6—*"He who began a good work in you, will perfect it until the day of Christ Jesus."*

B. The Difference-9:28g—". . . without reference to sin . . ."

Note: "Without reference to sin" literally means apart from sin or separate from sin. Christ will not be bearing the sin of many on Him as in His first coming. That sin has been taken care of based on the cross. Thankfully, Christ's Second Coming will have no more to do with sin.

Transition: Then what does this verse have to say about when He will return?

IV. QUESTION #4: WHEN WILL HE RETURN?-9:28d-e

A. The Time-9:28d—". . . will appear . . ."

"**will appear**"-(Future, Passive, Indicative, 3rd Person, Singular, οραω-Predictive) This verb demonstrates that at some future date, Christ will be made known or be experienced by the world at His Second Coming. The future tense of this verb for "appearing" suggests that it could happen at any moment. Therefore, His immanent return is a pressing and pending matter that should be considered by all.

Note: While the question of at what time is still up in the air, there is no question whatsoever that He will definitely return.

B. The Number-9:28e—". . . a second time . . ."

Note: As explained earlier, this is the second time He is appearing. The first advent included His birth, life, death, and resurrection on the earth. While others like many of the Jews are still anticipating the first coming of the Messiah, believers are expecting the Second Coming of Christ Jesus.

Transition: Who then will enjoy the benefits of Christ's Second Coming?

V. QUESTION #5: WHOM IS HE RETURNING FOR?-9:28h-i

A. Who are they?-9:28h—". . . to those who eagerly await . . ."

"who eagerly await"-(Present, Middle, Participle, Dative, Masculine, Plural, απεκεχομαι-Substantival) This participle describes a continual action, i.e., "to those who are currently and continuously awaiting." The middle voice of this verbal adjective emphasizes that it is a personal and pending action.

Note: Jesus is not coming for everyone. Instead, He is returning only for those who are awaiting Him (those who are saved and have a reason in the first place to anticipate His return).

Illustration: When I was in grade school, most of the time I would ride the bus home. However, there were several days when someone, either my dad or my mom would pick me up. The whole day long I anticipated their return and after the last bell rang I stood outside on the curb and waited patiently. They were coming to pick me up, not the other kids, not those riding the bus, not those staying after school. They were coming for me because I belonged to them. I am their son. Because I belonged to them, I eagerly awaited the revelation of their van to come zipping around the corner. This describes how believers anticipate Christ's return for them. They wait because they know He's coming for them. Others do not wait because they do not belong to Him.

B. What are they waiting for?-9:28i—". . . Him."

Note: This verse is held together by two bookends that have everything to do with Christ. "Christ" is coming and it is "He" who believers are waiting for. Christ and His work envelope the entire doctrine of the Second Coming. It is based in His work, it is He that will return and it is He that His children anticipate. Notice that it is not heaven that is being awaited. It is not eternal life. The believer anticipates Christ the most.

Reflection: If heaven for you didn't include seeing your family members that have died ahead of you, if it didn't include the matchless beauty and splendor we dream about, If heaven didn't include the

132

precious treasures and rewards promised, If when we gained heaven we gained only Christ, would that be enough to satisfy you? Would that be enough to give you hope? His Second Coming isn't about gaining heaven, it is about gaining Christ fully now with the body along with the soul.

Conclusion: How do these questions and answers play out in our own lives? While many are up in arms about the end of the world, Christians are those who are waiting eagerly for the hope that is not yet realized. We've heard it said, "He's coming, are you ready?" but perhaps the better thought would read, "He's coming, are you waiting?" Though this passage may not answer all of our questions about Christ's Second Coming, it answers what is most important. We have learned from Hebrews 9:28 that it is Christ who will return, His return is based on His first coming, His return is for the salvation of our bodies, His return is definite and immanent, and He is returning for those who are waiting for Him. By means of application today may I humbly suggest that we live lives as if we were waiting for Christ. May we eagerly anticipate and long for Him to come and save us from the flesh that still entangles us. May we strive to share the hope we have with those who have no one to pick them up and run the risk of being left behind. It has always been about Christ, and it will be on that day when the greatest return of all will take place. Are you ready? Are you waiting?

Printed in the United States
By Bookmasters